Ideal home cooking

Ideal home
COO

king

Paul and Jeanne Rankin

BOXTREE

Acknowledgements **Photography** All food photography © copyright Gus Filgate except those on pages 11 top, 42, 55 bottom, 62, 79, 83, 95, 98 bottom, 127 top left & bottom right, 138, 146, 167, 182 © copyright Graham Kirk. Photographs of Paul and Jeanne Rankin by Khara Pringle/Christopher Hill Photographic pp 3, 8, 9. **Food Stylists** Antonia Gaunt pages 6 top left, 10, 11 bottom right, 14, 35, 43 bottom right, 46 bottom left & bottom right, 63, 71 bottom left, 78 bottom, 91, 102 bottom right, 107 bottom, 111 bottom right, 114, 126, 142, 154, 155, 166, 178. Julie Rogers pages 2 right, 3 right, 6 bottom left, 6 top right, 6 bottom right, 11 bottom left, 15, 22, 23, 26, 27, 30, 31, 38 top, 38 bottom left, 39, 42, 43 bottom left, 46 top, 51, 62, 66, 67, 71 top, 71 bottom right, 75, 78 top, 79, 87, 90 bottom, 95, 98, 99, 102 top & bottom left, 107 top, 111 left & top right, 115, 119, 123, 127 all, 130, 131, 135, 139, 143, 146, 147, 151, 159, 163, 171, 174, 179, 182, 183. **Home Economists** Linda Tubby pages 12, 13, 15, 21, 24, 26, 27, 29, 30, 31, 32, 36, 37, 40, 41, 44, 45, 47, 48, 49, 50, 51, 54, 57, 60, 64, 65, 66, 67, 68, 69, 73, 76, 80, 81, 85, 86, 88, 91, 93, 94, 96,101, 103, 104, 106, 108, 109, 113, 114, 116, 117, 118, 120, 121, 124, 130, 131, 132, 133, 134 all, 136 bottom, 137, 139, 141, 144, 145,150, 152,158, 162,168, 170, 172, 174, 177, 180, 181. Louise Pickford pages 14, 16, 20, 25, 33, 34, 70, 72, 74, 77, 84, 100, 105, 110, 112, 122, 128, 135, 136 top, 140, 148, 153, 156, 160, 176, Gilliam MacLaurin pages 28, 53, 61, 89, 165. Jane Suthering 52, 97, 125, 129,164.

Photographs on title page are (left to right): Grilled Courgettes with Garlic, Chickpeas and Fresh Marjoram, Bloody Mary Gazpacho and Mascarpone Mousse with Roasted Apricots. Photographs on page 6 are (clockwise): Smoked Salmon Carpaccio with Horseradish Cream, Medley of Seafood with Herbs and Garlic, Moroccan Spiced Lamb Kebabs and Penne with Mushroom Pesto and Asparagus.

First published in 1998 by Boxtree

an imprint of Macmillan Publishers Ltd

25 Eccleston Place London SW1W 9NF

and Basingstoke

Associated companies throughout the world

ISBN 0 7522 2428 X

Text copyright © Paul and Jeanne Rankin 1998

The right of Paul and Jeanne Rankin to be identified as the authors of this work has been asserted by them in accordance with the Copyright, Designs and Patents Act 1988.

A CIP catalogue record for this book is available from the British Library

Designed by Roger Hammond

Typeset by Florencetype
Printed and bound in Italy by New InterLitho

Ideal Home is published monthly by IPC Magazines Limited, King's Reach Tower, Stamford Street, London SE1 9LS. For subscription enquiries and overseas orders call 01444-445555 (fax no. 01444-445599). Please send all correspondence to: IPC Magazines Limited, Oakfield House, 35 Perrymount Road, Haywards Heath, West Sussex RH16 3DH. Alternatively, you can call the subscription credit card hotline (UK orders only) on; 01622 778778.

9 8 7 6 5 4 3 2 1

contents

introduction

Food has never been more exciting or inspiring than it is right now. Across the world winds of change have been sweeping kitchens clear of weary and worn-out methods of cooking, and welcoming new concepts which bring together styles, techniques and flavours from a huge variety of national cuisines. And it's happening everywhere – from Australia, California, Hong Kong and across Europe to right here in the UK.

When asked to define our style of cooking, we would have to say that we heartily encompass this excitement of global cooking, borrowing flavours and methods from our favourite cuisines around the world. But our improvisations always build on a solid grounding in the classical and traditional techniques of cooking – in essence, our food is simply prepared but cleverly combined. We feel that good food should be intriguing, with texture and colour to please the eye and an abundance of taste to please the palate.

Although we have great respect for the 'temple of gastronomy' offerings of many upmarket restaurants, at Roscoff, our restaurant in Belfast, we have set out to achieve something very different. We believe that rather than creating a dish which looks beautiful at the expense of real flavour, the tastes should zip about and play with your senses, textures should tease and tantalise and the dish should look so appealing that it almost jumps off the plate. We also like to use the seasons as our guide as we still believe that food actually tastes better when it's in season or, if you're lucky, grown locally.

It's also important that food fits into our hectic lifestyles – we don't

Today's food is fun, eating it should be a pleasure, and now preparing it can be too. Enjoy.

have time to spend hours in our kitchen at home each day so why should we expect anyone else to? And just because time is a factor, wholesomeness and taste needn't be sacrificed. Homemade soups can be quick and healthy, a salad a complete meal without dirtied pans, and pastas and risottos the perfect comfort food, easy to prepare for any number and ideal for kids. Yet for the special occasion, it's great to go

*W*e've been writing our monthly collection of recipes for **Ideal Home** magazine for two years, and many have been developed from popular dishes served in our restaurant or from our own personal favourites at home. Our aim has been to make all the recipes suitable for people with a wide variety of kitchen skills. The recipes have been tested by us in our home kitchen, as well as by **Ideal Home**, and every one is easy to follow. Don't be afraid to substitute items if certain ingredients aren't available or, for example, your fishmonger suggests you should substitute a fantastic lobster for out-of-season prawns. We've also included the fat and calorie content for each recipe for, although we think you should be able to indulge once in a while, we do like to keep an eye on the nutritional value of our recipes.

the extra distance and make that special something. All the love and effort that goes into a meal is so often appreciated long after the event – we always think it's the essence of a generous spirit, a sharing of one's self.

Today's food is fun, eating it should be a pleasure, and now preparing it can be too. Enjoy.

Fish soup with chilli and coriander page 17

soups

Above: Watercress soup page 16

Far left; Chicken soup with
cannellini beans page 20

Left: Roast aubergine soup
with fresh coriander page12

Roast aubergine soup with fresh coriander

This spicy vegetable soup will certainly revive appetites at the end of the day. How hot you have it is up to you. Serrano chillies – red or green – are pretty fiery (you can use either colour). But if you can't get hold of them use a single Thai chilli, instead, but beware – they're very hot indeed.

1 medium large aubergine, cut into 1 cm (½ in) dice

2 tbsp vegetable oil

25 g (1 oz) butter

1 large onion, finely chopped

2 cloves of garlic, chopped

1–3 serrano chillies, finely sliced

1 tsp fresh ginger, chopped

1 tsp curry powder

1 tsp ground coriander seeds

1 tsp ground cumin seeds

400 ml (14 fl oz) tin of coconut milk

650 ml (22 fl oz) chicken stock

2 tbsp Thai fish sauce

4–6 tbsp lemon or lime juice

3 tbsp chopped fresh coriander

■ In a heavy frying pan, gently fry the aubergine in the vegetable oil over a moderate heat for about 10 minutes until the aubergine is just tender.

■ Meanwhile, melt the butter in a large saucepan and sweat the onion, garlic, chillies and spices for about 5 minutes. Add the aubergine, coconut milk, chicken stock and fish sauce, and simmer for 5 minutes. Season to taste.

■ Add the lemon or lime juice (you'll probably need more lemon than lime), then stir in the fresh coriander. Serve immediately.

Serves 4–6

120 cals per portion

8 g fat per portion

Onion soup with cider and stilton butter

The cider adds a nice bit of acidity to this long-standing favourite, while the Stilton butter adds a smooth, rich flavour.

2 tbsp butter
1 kg (2¼ lb) onions, roughly
   chopped
500 ml (18 fl oz) medium-dry cider
1 tbsp cider vinegar
Pinch of dried thyme
1 small bay leaf
2 litres (3½ pt) chicken stock
225 g (8 oz) potato, peeled and diced
Salt and freshly ground black pepper

STILTON BUTTER
4 tbsp butter, room temperature
2 tbsp single cream
4 tbsp Stilton (or Cashel Blue),
   crumbled, room temperature
1 tbsp chopped parsley
1 tbsp chives, snipped
Onion slices fried in butter and
   chervil to garnish

★The Stilton butter can be made in larger quantities and stored in the freezer. It makes an excellent spread for hors d'œuvres.

■ Melt the butter in a heavy saucepan, add the onions and cook gently over a medium heat for 15 minutes or until soft and lightly browned. Add the cider and cider vinegar and boil until reduced by about a half. Add the thyme, bay leaf, chicken stock, potato and a little salt. Bring to a simmer and cook for about 15 minutes over a low heat.

■ Remove the bay leaf and purée the soup in a blender or food processor until smooth. Season to taste.

■ To make the Stilton butter, mix all the ingredients together in a bowl until they are well blended.

■ To serve, ladle the hot soup into warm bowls. Add 1 tbsp of the Stilton butter to each bowl and garnish with the fried onion slices and chervil.

Serves 6
258 cals per portion
14 g fat per portion

Celeriac soup with truffle oil

A simple and hearty soup made rather glamorous by the addition of truffle oil. Although it is expensive, the oil is powerfully flavoured and a little goes a long way.

25–40 g (1–1½ oz) butter
1 medium to large onion, weighing about 225 g (8 oz), sliced
1 celeriac bulb, weighing 600–700 g (1¼–1½ lb), peeled and cut into 2 cm (¾ in) dice
1.5 litres (2½ pt) chicken stock
Salt and freshly ground white pepper

GARNISH
3 tbsp truffle oil
6 tbsp lightly whipped cream (optional)
Lightly toasted pine nuts or a few croûtons
2 tbsp chopped parsley

■ Melt the butter over a medium heat in a large saucepan and gently cook the onion slices for about 10 minutes, stirring regularly until they just start to colour. Add the diced celeriac, chicken stock and a little salt to the pan and bring to the boil. Skim off any foam that rises to the surface, turn the heat down low and simmer gently for 30 minutes.

■ Purée the soup in a blender or food processor to a smooth consistency and adjust the seasoning to taste with salt and white pepper.

■ To serve, ladle the soup into warmed bowls, drizzle each with a little truffle oil and, if you like, a spoonful of whipped cream. Sprinkle the pine nuts or croûtons and chopped parsley over the top.

Serves 6
217 cals per portion
20 g fat per portion

Bloody Mary gazpacho

A great recipe to have on hand for when you come across superbly flavoured tomatoes. It can be served either as an aperitif or a first course.

2 cloves of garlic, finely chopped

3–4 celery sticks, finely sliced

500 g (1 lb 2 oz) unpeeled ripe tomatoes, quartered, or 500 ml (16¾ fl oz) passata

100 g (3½ oz) onion, chopped

300 ml (10 fl oz) tomato juice

2–4 tbsp hot chilli sauce

Juice of 2 limes

100 ml (3½ fl oz) Worcestershire sauce

1 tsp celery salt

Tabasco to taste

Vodka to taste (optional)

2 tbsp extra virgin olive oil

4 celery sticks and herb sprigs to garnish

■ Put all the ingredients, except the oil and garnish, into a food processor and blend until smooth. Pass the mixture through a fine sieve, season and chill.

■ Transfer the soup to serving dishes with plenty of ice. Drizzle over the oil, and garnish with celery sticks and herb sprigs to serve.

Serves 4

114 cals per portion

6 g fat per portion

Watercress soup

This soup can be served warm or chilled. Crunchy croûtons are a great garnish on their own, but for a treat add the optional chopped egg.

170 g (6 oz) uncooked potatoes, peeled and diced
Salt and freshly ground black pepper
400 g (14 oz) watercress
1 tbsp vegetable oil

CROUTONS
3 thick slices of white bread, crusts discarded
100 ml (3½ fl oz) light olive oil

GARNISH
120 ml (4 fl oz) double cream
Watercress leaves
Mixed peppercorns, crushed
3 hard-boiled eggs, chopped (optional)

■ Place the potatoes in a heavy-based pan with 500 ml (18 fl oz) cold, salted water and bring to the boil. Lower the heat and simmer until tender. Meanwhile, trim and remove any thicker stalks and yellow leaves from the watercress.

■ Heat the vegetable oil in a large pan, add the watercress and cook for 1 minute – do not cook longer as it will lose its colour. Add the potatoes plus their cooking water and cook over a medium heat for a further 2 minutes.

■ Remove the mixture from the heat, blend in a liquidiser, then pass through a fine sieve. Season to taste with salt and freshly ground black pepper.

■ If the soup is too thick at this stage, dilute it with ice-cold water until it reaches its desired consistency. The cold water will also help it to keep its green colour. Set aside and leave to cool.

■ To make the croûtons, cut the bread into 1 cm (½ in) cubes. Heat the oil in a frying pan over a medium to high heat. When the oil is hot, add the bread and sauté quickly until just golden. Drain the croûtons on kitchen paper to remove excess oil.

■ Serve the soup hot or chilled with a swirl of double cream and a handful of croûtons. Garnish each bowl with watercress leaves and crushed peppercorns. For a more substantial course, sprinkle cold, hard-boiled eggs over the soup before serving.

Serves 4
492 cals per portion
42 g fat per portion

Fish soup with chilli and coriander

This quick and simple version of the classic fish soup offers the cook two variations: you can purée the base and add some cream to give an elegantly smooth soup, or omit the cream and leave the soup chunky for a more substantial meal.

25 g (1 oz) butter

1 large onion, weighing about 300 g (10½ oz), finely chopped

1 stick of celery, finely sliced

125g (4 oz) button mushrooms, sliced

3 tomatoes, cut into 1 cm (½ in) dice

1 tbsp tomato paste

Pinch of saffron

1 tbsp harissa (or other hot chilli paste)

1 litre (1¾ pt) fish stock or chicken stock

Salt and freshly ground black pepper

450 g (1 lb) mixed fish fillets, such as hake, cod, monkfish, prawns and salmon, cut into 1 cm (½ in) dice

125 ml (4 fl oz) whipping cream (optional)

4 tbsp fresh coriander, chopped, to garnish

■ Melt the butter in a large saucepan and cook the onion, celery and mushrooms over a medium heat, stirring occasionally, for about 10 minutes until soft.

■ Add the tomatoes, tomato paste, saffron, harissa, fish or chicken stock and a little salt. Bring to the boil, then skim off any surface foam. Reduce the heat to a simmer and cook for 15 minutes until the vegetables are soft. This is the stage at which to purée the mixture in a food processor then return it to the pan if you want a smooth-textured soup. Taste and adjust seasoning.

■ To serve, bring the soup to the boil and add all the fish. If you've puréed the soup, stir in most of the cream, saving a few spoonfuls for the final presentation. Bring the soup just back to the boil, then remove from heat and leave to stand for 5 minutes.

■ Ladle into warmed soup plates and drizzle the remaining cream over the creamed soup. Sprinkle the fresh coriander over the top and serve immediately.

Serves 8

171 cals per portion

12 g fat per portion

Carrot soup with mussels and dill

Carrots and mussels may not be recognized immediately as perfect partners, but they really do go very well together. It's their sublime sweetness that makes them work. You can substitute the mussels with other shellfish, such as cockles or scallops, if you prefer.

55 g (2 oz) butter
2 medium onions, chopped
Pinch of curry powder
Salt and freshly ground black pepper
450 g (1 lb) carrots
1 litre (1¾ pt) chicken or vegetable
 stock or water
1 kg (2¼ lb) mussels
Small bunch of dill
150 ml (5 fl oz) dry white wine
Squeeze of lemon juice
4 tbsp double cream
Dill sprigs to garnish

■ In a large pot, melt the butter over a medium heat and sweat the onions for about 10 minutes. Add the curry powder, a good pinch of salt and the carrots and continue to cook for 10 minutes. Add the stock or water and simmer for 15–20 minutes, until the carrots are very tender. Remove from the heat and purée in a blender or liquidizer.

■ While the soup is cooking, wash the mussels in plenty of cold water, pulling away and discarding the hairy beards. Discard any mussels that are open, or do not close when tapped with a knife, as it means they are dead and therefore not fresh. Pick the dill leaves from the stems, roughly chop the leaves and set aside.

■ Put the dill stems in a large pot with the white wine and bring to a vigorous boil. Add the mussels, cover tightly with a lid and cook for 4–5 minutes, or until the mussels have all opened. (Again, discard any that will not open.) Drain into a large colander, catching all the juices in a bowl underneath. Strain the juices through a fine sieve and add to the carrot soup. As soon as the mussels are cool enough to handle, remove them from their shells. Reserve a few in their shells to use as a garnish.

■ Taste the soup for seasoning, adding a little more salt or pepper if necessary. Add a squeeze of lemon juice and the chopped dill leaves.

■ To serve, divide the mussels equally among warm soup bowls. Ladle the hot soup on top and finish each with a spoonful of cream. Top with a

few sprigs of dill and one or two of the reserved
mussel shells. Serve immediately.

Serves 4

268 cals per portion

19 g fat per portion

Chicken soup with cannellini beans

The addition of cannellini beans gives this nutritious soup real substance and a good flavour.

1 litre (1¾ pt) water or chicken stock
4 chicken thighs (or 2 whole legs)
2 medium onions, finely chopped
1 tsp salt
2 cans cannellini beans
1 small bunch of parsley, chopped
125 ml (4 fl oz) double cream (optional)
Squeeze of lemon juice (optional)

■ Put the water or stock, chicken, onions, salt and 1 can of beans in a large saucepan. Bring to the boil and simmer gently for 40 minutes.

■ Remove the chicken from the saucepan and set aside to cool.

■ Take off the chicken meat from the bones and cut into small dice. Liquidize the soup in a blender or food processor and put back into the pan with the chicken meat. Add the remaining beans and the parsley. Simmer for 5 minutes, stir in the double cream (if using) and lemon juice and serve.

Serves 6
219 cals per portion
9.5 g fat per portion

Laksa noodle soup with tofu

In Indonesia and Malaysia, laksa is the name of a rice noodle dish, usually with a creamy curry or tart tamarind sauce. This recipe is of the first type, but rather than adding fish, shrimp or chicken we have added tofu, making this a wonderful vegetarian option.

310 g (11 oz) dried flat rice noodles
    (or egg noodles)
1 onion, roughly chopped
2 tbsp galangal (or ginger), grated
2 cloves of garlic, roughly chopped
2 lemon grass stalks, sliced
½ tsp crushed chillies
1 tbsp cashew nuts, roughly
    chopped
3 tbsp vegetable oil
1 tsp ground coriander
1 tsp paprika
1 tsp turmeric
½ tsp ground cumin
400 ml (14 fl oz) can coconut milk
850 ml (1½ pt) vegetable stock
2 tsp sugar
½ tsp salt

GARNISH
225 g (8 oz) tofu pieces (firm variety)
85 g (3 oz) fresh bean sprouts
85 g (3 oz) cooked green beans,
    finely sliced
4 spring onions, finely sliced
1 tbsp chopped fresh mint
1 tbsp chopped fresh coriander
1 lime, cut into wedges

■ Prepare the noodles according to the packet's instructions and keep to one side.

■ Place the onion, galangal, garlic, lemon grass, chillies and cashew nuts in a blender or food processor and purèe to a paste.

■ Heat the oil in a frying pan and stir-fry the paste for 2–3 minutes. Add the spices and cook for a further minute. Add the coconut milk, vegetable stock, sugar and salt and, finally, the tofu pieces.

■ To serve, divide the noodles and the remaining garnishes between the bowls, and ladle on the soup. Serve with a lime on the side.

Serves 4–6
442 cals per portion
15 g fat per portion

Smoked salmon eggs benedict page 32

starters

Smoked salmon with avocado frittata page 33

& light dishes

Grilled courgettes with garlic, chickpeas and fresh marjoram

A vegetarian starter where the ultra-fast cooking sears smoky flavour into the courgettes. These are served stacked on a sauce made by liquidizing a can of chickpeas. Cooking can't get simpler than this.

4 small, firm dark green courgettes

4 small, firm yellow courgettes

4 tbsp extra virgin olive oil

1½ cloves of garlic

1 tsp cracked black pepper

2 tbsp chopped fresh marjoram

400 g (14 oz) can chickpeas

1 tbsp lemon juice

Salt and freshly ground black pepper

★ This dish is just as good if you use fresh thyme leaves instead of marjoram.

■ Cut each courgette lengthways into 4. Mix with half the olive oil, 1 crushed clove of garlic, the black pepper and half the fresh marjoram. Leave the courgettes in this marinade for at least 30 minutes.

■ Drain the liquid from the chickpeas into a blender or food processor. Reserving 4 tbsp of the chickpeas, blend or process the rest with the chickpea liquid, remaining ½ clove of garlic, roughly chopped, and the lemon juice. Blend until smooth, adding cold water if necessary to thin to a pourable sauce consistency. Taste and season.

■ Pre-heat the grill to high. Season the courgettes with salt and cook under the grill for about 3 minutes until lightly charred.

■ To serve, arrange 2 courgette pieces parallel on each plate and put another 2 on top at right angles. Continue until you have built up 4 layers. Spoon the chickpea purée around the courgette stack, then garnish with a sprinkling of the remaining marjoram, the reserved chickpeas and a drizzle of oil. Serve at room temperature or slightly warm (the chickpea purée can be gently heated in a saucepan).

Serves 4

202 cals per portion

13.51 g fat per portion

Vegetable puff pizza

This is fun to serve as a starter or as a garnish to a main course, such as the lamb dish on page 100. If it's for a starter, sprinkle a few tablespoons of grated Parmesan or Gruyère cheese over the vegetables before baking.

150–175 g (5–6 oz) puff pastry
15 g (½ oz) butter
½ courgette, finely sliced
½ red pepper, seeded and sliced
½ red onion, finely sliced
4-5 button mushrooms, sliced
Salt and freshly ground black pepper
1 egg yolk, lightly beaten
Basil leaves to garnish

■ Roll out the pastry so it is 0.5 cm (¼ in) thick and chill in the fridge for at least 30 minutes. Meanwhile, pre-heat the oven to 190°C/375°F/Gas 5.

■ Cut a 20 cm (8 in) circle from the pastry and prick the whole surface evenly with a fork. Place on a baking sheet and cook in the oven for 10–15 minutes until nicely golden.

■ While the pastry is baking, sauté the vegetables in the butter until just wilted but not fully cooked. Season with salt and pepper.

■ Remove the pastry from the oven and lower the oven temperature to 180°C/350°F/Gas 4. Brush the pastry with egg yolk so that the vegetables don't stick and to stop the pastry from absorbing excess liquid from the vegetables.

■ Spread the vegetables evenly over the pastry and return to the oven for about 10 minutes until the pastry is puffed and golden and the vegetables are cooked. Garnish with basil and serve hot, cut into wedges.

Serves 4
217 cals per portion
15 g fat per portion

Fennel, onion and mushroom tarts

An unusual combination of vegetables flavours these savoury tartlets, held in a rich puff pastry and surrounded by a creamy sauce.

225 g (8 oz) puff pastry
175 g (6 oz) mixed mushrooms, such as chestnut, shitake and oyster
1 red onion
1 fennel bulb
6 cloves of garlic
Light olive oil
Salt and freshly ground black pepper
Fresh chives to garnish

SAUCE
100 ml (3½ fl oz) whipping cream
100 g (4 oz) unsalted butter, chilled and diced
1 tbsp lemon juice
1 tbsp fresh chives, snipped
1 tbsp flat-leaf parsley, chopped

■ Grease 4 x 10 cm (4 in) fluted loose-bottomed tartlet tins, about 3 cm (1¼ in) deep. Roll out the pastry to 3 mm (⅛ in) thick and use to line the tins. Prick the pastry bases well, then chill for at least 30 minutes.

■ Pre-heat the oven to 180°C/350°F/Gas 4. Cover each pastry base with greaseproof paper, fill with baking beans and bake for 15–20 minutes. Remove from the oven and take out the beans and paper. Return the pastry cases to the oven until cooked and light brown.

■ Increase the oven temperature to 220°C/425°F/Gas 7. Clean, cut and trim the mushrooms as necessary. Peel the onion, leaving the root intact, and cut into 8 wedges along the axis of the root. Trim the tops off the fennel, cut into quarters and cut out the root. Slice into 1 cm (½ in) chunks.

■ Blanch the fennel in boiling salted water for 2 minutes, drain and wipe dry with kitchen paper. Using the flat of a knife, lightly crush the garlic cloves in their skins. Place the garlic on a baking sheet with the vegetables, drizzle with olive oil and toss gently. Season, then bake for 10–15 minutes, or until cooked and tinged brown.

■ To make the sauce, bring the cream to the boil in a small pan. Whisk in the butter, add the lemon juice and herbs and season. Remove the garlic cloves from the vegetables and tease out the roast garlic from the skins. Mash 2 of the cloves with the point of a knife, add to the sauce and whisk again. Add the remaining garlic back into the vegetables.

■ Fill the pre-baked pastry shells with the vegetable mixture. Heat for 1–2 minutes in the oven, then serve on warmed plates surrounded with sauce and garnished with chives.

Serves 4

542 cals per portion

47 g fat per portion

Mushroom bruschetta with grilled chicory

A mixture of wild mushrooms makes this dish very special, but if you can't find wild ones, use whatever mushrooms are available in your local shops.

225g (8 oz) mushrooms
2 cloves of garlic
4 tbsp light olive oil
1 tbsp chopped fresh parsley
2 large heads of chicory
Salt and freshly ground black
   pepper
4 slices baguette or country bread
4 tbsp balsamic vinegar
2 tbsp extra virgin olive oil
Shavings of Parmesan and sprigs of
   parsley to garnish

■ Trim and clean the mushrooms. Chop 1 garlic clove very finely and cut the other in half. Heat a large pan over high heat and sauté the mushrooms in 3 tbsp light olive oil. When they are lightly browned, add the chopped garlic and, after 1 minute, remove from the heat and add the chopped parsley.

■ Heat a ridged grill pan over moderate heat, cut the chicory lengthways into quarters, brush with a little light olive oil, season and cook for about 3 minutes each side until well marked and almost tender.

■ Toast the bread and rub one side of each slice with the cut garlic. Arrange the slices on warmed plates, top with mushrooms and 2 pieces each of chicory, drizzle with balsamic vinegar and a little extra virgin oil and top with shavings of Parmesan and sprigs of parsley.

Serves 4

299 cals per portion

19 g fat per portion

Pizza tart

A versatile dish with familiar pizza flavours in a deep and creamy tart case – great for a summer buffet.

350 g (12 oz) unsweetened shortcrust pastry
½ red pepper
½ yellow pepper
3 tbsp light olive oil
1 red onion
1 courgette
½ aubergine
Salt and freshly ground black pepper
2 egg yolks
1 egg
250 ml (9 fl oz) whipping cream
1 clove of garlic, finely chopped
2 tsp freshly chopped thyme
300 g (10½ oz) goat's cheese, crumbled

■ Pre-heat the oven to 180°C/350°F/Gas 4. Grease a 25 cm (10 in) tart tin and roll out the pastry to line the tin. Chill for 20 minutes while you heat the oven, then blind bake the pastry case for 15–20 minutes until golden brown.

■ Meanwhile, rub the pepper halves with a little olive oil and roast under a very hot grill – or in a hot oven – until the skin is blistered and blackened. Peel, de-seed and cut each piece into 6 strips.

■ Cut the onion and courgette into 2 cm (¾ in) cubes and the aubergine into 2.5 cm (1 in) cubes. Season and brush the vegetables with olive oil then grill them separately until cooked through – about 5–6 minutes for the onion and courgette, a little longer for the aubergine.

■ Whisk the egg yolks and whole egg together. Beat in the cream, garlic and thyme, and season. Spread the crumbled goat's cheese and the vegetables over the base of the tart and pour in the egg mixture.

■ Return to the oven and cook for 40–45 minutes, until just set. Cool for 10 minutes before serving.

Serves 6–8
501 cals per portion
39.42 g fat per portion

Goat's cheese pâté with red onion marmalade

A little beetroot and a slow simmer in red wine bring out both the sweetness and the deep ruby colour of red onions. This 'marmalade' offsets the pale, salty creaminess of peppered goat's cheese laced with green herbs.

500 g (1 lb 2 oz) goat's cheese
150 ml (5 fl oz) whipping cream
1 sachet gelatine
2 tbsp lemon juice
1½ tsp cracked black pepper
2 tbsp chopped parsley
2 tbsp chopped chives
2 tbsp chopped basil

RED ONION MARMALADE
2 medium-sized red onions, finely
  chopped
1 tbsp light olive oil
1 medium-sized beetroot, grated
½ bottle red wine
2 tbsp balsamic vinegar
1½ tbsp honey
1 tsp salt

GARNISH
Chive and parsley sprigs
3 tbsp chopped walnut kernels
6 tbsp walnut oil

■ Break up the goat's cheese, peeling if necessary, and leave it to stand in a warm place. Bring the whipping cream to the boil, sprinkle on the gelatine and lemon juice, and whisk for at least 1 minute until the gelatine has fully dissolved. Add to the goat's cheese, together with the cracked black pepper and chopped herbs, and mix thoroughly.

■ Lay out a sheet of cling-film, then spread the cheese mixture along it and shape into a log. Roll up the cling-film to hold the shape and refrigerate for 4 hours.

■ To make the marmalade, cook the red onions in the oil in a stainless-steel pan over a gentle heat for 10 minutes, stirring regularly. Add the remaining ingredients. Bring to the boil and cook slowly until the red wine has reduced and has been almost completely absorbed. This will take about 30–40 minutes. Tip the mixture into a bowl and leave to cool. Season to taste, if necessary.

■ To serve, remove the cling-film from the pâté and cut into 1 cm (½ in) slices. Arrange 2 slices in the centre of each plate and surround with spoonfuls of the red onion marmalade. Garnish with herbs and chopped walnuts then drizzle with the walnut oil. Serve with fresh crusty bread.

Serves 6
540 cals per portion
43.78 g fat per portion

Warm potato and goat's cheese flan

A real winner for vegetarians. To our taste, potato and goat's cheese go so well together – the potato cuts the richness of the cheese and cream to produce a silky, yet rustic texture.

200 g (7 oz) potatoes, peeled and roughly cut
125 ml (4½ fl oz) milk
125 ml (4½ fl oz) whipping cream
Salt and freshly ground black pepper
150 g (5 oz) firm goat's cheese
3 egg yolks
15 g (½ oz) butter, softened

GARNISH
Small bunch of rocket leaves, whole or sliced, plus flowers if available
8 anchovies, soaked in milk for 30 minutes
12 black olives, roughly chopped
1–2 tbsp good quality capers, drained and rinsed
4 tbsp extra virgin olive oil

■ Pre-heat the oven to 160°C/325°F/Gas 3. Cook the potatoes in salted boiling water until just tender. Drain and return to the pan with the milk and cream. Simmer for 4–5 minutes until the liquid thickens slightly. Remove from the heat and mash roughly with a potato masher. Season with salt and pepper and allow to cool for a few minutes. Stir in the crumbled goat's cheese and the egg yolks.

■ Generously butter 4 x 150 ml (5 fl oz) ramekins or ovenproof cups, and pour in the potato and goat's cheese mixture. Place the ramekins or cups in a deep roasting tin and pour boiling water into the tin so it comes halfway up the sides of the moulds.

■ Bake in the centre of the oven for 45–55 minutes or until just set. Remove the moulds from the roasting tin and allow to cool for 15–20 minutes before serving. Alternatively, you can cook them well before needed and simply reheat in the water bath just before serving.

■ Turn the flans out on to plates and garnish with rocket leaves and flowers, anchovies, olives and capers. Drizzle with olive oil and serve with grilled focaccia bread.

Serves 4
474 cals per portion
42 g fat per portion

Goat's cheese and potato tart with parma ham

This well-flavoured tart is a satisfying starter with salad and a thin slice of Italy's finest ham. Cheddar or Gruyère can be used instead of goat's cheese.

Butter for greasing

225 g (8 oz) ready-made shortcrust pastry, defrosted if frozen

15 g (½ oz butter)

1 small onion, finely chopped

225 g (8 oz) waxy potatoes, cooked, peeled and cut into 1 cm (½ in) slices

Salt and freshly ground black pepper

125 g (4 oz) goat's cheese, crumbled

2 eggs plus 1 extra yolk

240 ml (8 fl oz) single cream

1 tbsp finely chopped parsley

2 tbsp snipped chives

SALAD

100 g (3½ oz) mixed salad leaves

4 tbsp vinaigrette

8 slices Parma ham

■ Heat the oven to 180°C/350°F/Gas 4 and grease a 20 cm (8 in) diameter tart tin.

■ Roll out the pastry, line the tin and chill in the fridge for 20 minutes. Bake blind for 10–15 minutes until the pastry edges are light golden brown. Remove the baking beans and set the pastry base aside to cool.

■ Melt the butter in a small pan and cook the onion for about 5 minutes until soft, stirring regularly. Transfer to a large bowl with the potatoes, season generously and add the crumbled cheese.

■ In a medium bowl whisk the eggs and yolks together well, add the cream, herbs and ½ tsp salt and whisk gently until smooth, then pour over the potato and cheese mixture and stir.

■ Spread the filling in the pastry case and bake in the oven for about 40 minutes until the filling is set. Leave to cool for 15 minutes before serving.

■ To serve, place a wedge of tart on each plate. Toss the salad leaves with the vinaigrette and put a little pile of salad topped with a slice of ham beside each slice of tart.

Serves 8

233 cals per portion

18 g fat

Smoked salmon eggs benedict

This elegant dish makes a brilliant brunch centrepiece.

250 g (9 oz) puff pastry
1 egg yolk mixed with 1 tbsp cold water
25 g (1 oz) butter
250g (9 oz) spinach, washed
Salt and freshly ground black pepper
150 g (5 oz) sliced smoked salmon
8 large, very fresh free-range eggs
Chives and tarragon leaves to garnish

BUTTER SAUCE
100 ml (3½ fl oz) whipping cream
100 g (3½ oz) unsalted butter
1 tbsp Dijon mustard
1 tbsp lemon juice
1 tbsp snipped fresh chives
1 tbsp chopped fresh tarragon

■ Roll the pastry to 0.5 cm (¼ in) thickness, cover and chill in the fridge for at least 1 hour.

■ Pre-heat the oven to 200°C/400°/Gas 6. Cut 8 x 8 cm (3 in) circles from the pastry, put them on a baking sheet and carefully brush the top of each with the egg yolk wash. Bake for 10 minutes, reduce the oven temperature to 170°C/325°F/Gas 3 and bake for a further 10 minutes, then remove from the oven and leave to cool.

■ Heat 25 g (1 oz) butter in a large frying pan over moderate heat and, when it foams, add the spinach and a little salt and pepper. Stir occasionally until the leaves are tender and bright green. Drain off any excess liquid and keep warm. Cut the smoked salmon into broad strips, discarding any dark pieces.

■ Bring a shallow saucepan of water to the boil and poach the eggs. Lift them out with a slotted spoon, trim the ragged edges and drain on a clean tea towel.

■ To make the sauce, bring the cream to the boil in a small pan, whisk in the butter, remove from the heat and whisk in the mustard, lemon juice, herbs and seasoning.

■ To serve, put a little spinach on top of each pastry circle and arrange smoked salmon on top. Put them in the oven for a minute, then put 2 on each plate, top each with a poached egg and pour the sauce over. Garnish with chives and tarragon.

Serves 4
827 cals per portion
67 g fat per portion

Smoked salmon with avocado frittata

The classic combination of smoked salmon and eggs has been given a modern twist, with influences from Italy and Mexico.

1 large avocado

4 tbsp lime (or lemon) juice

2 tbsp butter

1 small onion, finely chopped

4 eggs

Salt and freshly ground black pepper

4 tbsp snipped chives

225 g (8 oz) smoked salmon

1 tomato, peeled, seeded and diced

Fresh coriander and long chives to
   garnish

Chilli oil (optional)

AVOCADO VINAIGRETTE

⅓ avocado (from main ingredients)

2 tbsp lime (or lemon) juice (from
   main ingredients)

1 tbsp cooked onion (from main
   ingredients)

2 tbsp chopped fresh coriander
   (optional)

55 ml (2 fl oz) light olive oil

Few drops of Tabasco, or a pinch of
   chilli powder or fresh chilli

■ Peel and dice two-thirds of the avocado and toss in 2 tbsp of the lime or lemon juice. Heat the butter in a non-stick frying pan and gently fry the onion for 3 minutes. Remove about 1 tbsp of the cooked onion and set aside for the vinaigrette.

■ Whisk the eggs with a good pinch of salt and pepper, and add to the pan. Cook the eggs quite slowly, stirring often until curds form.

■ Stir in the avocado and 2 tbsp of the chives, then gently pat the mixture into a flat shape. Cover the pan, turn the heat down and cook for 3–4 minutes until the egg is firmly set.

■ To make the vinaigrette, place the remaining avocado, onion and other ingredients in a blender, and pulse to a smooth purée. Alternatively, mash together and push through a fine sieve with the back of a spoon. Season to taste.

■ To serve, turn the frittata on to a clean chopping board and cut into 4 wedges. Place a wedge on each serving plate. Arrange a tumble of smoked salmon beside or on top of each frittata and spoon the vinaigrette around each one. Garnish with the tomato, coriander, chives and chilli oil, if using. Serve hot or cold.

Serves 4

442 cals per portion

37.5 g fat per portion

Smoked salmon carpaccio with horseradish cream

Classic carpaccio is made with very thinly sliced raw beef, but we've borrowed the term to define a presentation of salmon covering the plate as a lining for jewel-like garnishings. Extravagantly beautiful, this would make a sophisticated starter to Christmas dinner, or you could present it on a large platter at a buffet party.

300 g (10½ oz) thinly sliced smoked salmon

1 small avocado, cut into 1 cm (½ in) dice

1 cooked beetroot, cut into 1 cm (½ in) dice

1 tbsp snipped chives

1 tbsp chopped fresh dill

Fresh chives to garnish

SAUCE

2–3 tbsp whipping cream

2 tbsp creamed horseradish

1 tsp Dijon mustard

½ tsp sugar

Salt and freshly ground white pepper

■ Trim the salmon slices, discarding any dark pieces. Carefully spread the fish slices into neat circles to fill the centre of 4 serving plates.

■ To make the sauce, bring the cream to the boil in a small saucepan, remove from the heat and stir in the horseradish, mustard, sugar and a little salt and pepper.

■ To serve, scatter each plate of salmon with diced avocado and beetroot. Spatter with the horseradish sauce and sprinkle the snipped chives and chopped fresh dill over the top. Garnish with the remaining chives.

Serves 4
204 cals per portion
12 g fat per portion

Fried prawns with chilli tomato dressing

Crisp and thoroughly spicy, these prawns with their hottish sauce make a light starter.

2 spring onions, finely sliced

1 tsp minced garlic

2 tsp finely chopped ginger

Vegetable oil for frying

1 tbsp rice wine vinegar or white wine vinegar

1 tsp crushed dried chillies or 2 fresh green chillies, finely chopped

3 plum tomatoes, peeled, seeded and diced

1 tbsp tomato ketchup

2 tbsp finely chopped fresh basil

16 raw king prawns

1 egg white

2 tbsp whipping cream

150 g (5 oz) plain flour

1½ tsp salt

1 tsp ground white pepper

2 tsp chilli powder

2 tsp curry powder

Oil for deep-frying

Spring onions to garnish

■ Cook the spring onion, garlic and ginger in warmed vegetable oil for 1 minute or until very pale golden. Carefully add the vinegar, chillies, tomatoes and ketchup, bring to the boil and cook for 1 minute, then remove from the heat and add the basil.

■ Shell the prawns, leaving on the tails (they look better). Cut along the curved back of each prawn and remove any dark vein.

■ Whisk together the egg white and cream. In a separate dish, mix the flour, salt, pepper, chilli powder and curry powder. Heat the oil for deep-frying.

■ Toss the prawns lightly in the spiced flour, then in the egg and cream, mixing thoroughly until covered with a sticky coating. Return them to the flour, rubbing some on each. Shake off excess flour.

■ Fry the prawns and drain on kitchen paper. Serve immediately on warm plates with the chilli tomato dressing. Garnish with spring onions slit lengthways and soaked in iced water to make them curl.

Serves 4

407 cals per portion

20 g fat per portion

Sautéed prawns with potato and basil cream

These can be served as a light first course or as a canapé

12 large raw king prawns, peeled

12 cloves of garlic, unpeeled

2 tbsp butter

2 tbsp oil

100 ml (3½ fl oz) double cream

Salt and freshly ground black pepper

2 tbsp chopped fresh basil

2 medium-sized waxy potatoes,
   cooked in their skins and peeled

■ Pre-heat the oven to 200°C/400°F/Gas 6. Make an incision along the rounded back of the prawns and remove the dark vein. Using your fingers, press open (butterfly) the prawns slightly.

■ Place the garlic cloves in a pan, cover with water and bring to the boil. Boil for just 1 minute, then cool under running water. Peel the cloves. Place the garlic in the centre of a sheet of foil, adding ½ tbsp butter and ½ tbsp oil. Pull up the corners of the foil to make a small parcel, place in a baking dish and cook in the oven for 30 minutes.

■ Boil the cream for 1–2 minutes, until just slightly thickened. Add the garlic and its juices from the foil pack, and blend in a liquidizer with salt and pepper to taste. (If you don't have a liquidizer, mash the garlic with a fork and whisk it into the cream.) Stir in the basil just before serving.

■ Cut the potatoes into 12 even-sized slices and fry in 1 tbsp oil and 1 tbsp butter until golden brown. Remove from the pan and set aside. Add the remaining oil and butter to the pan with the prawns. Season to taste with salt and pepper. Cook the prawns quickly over a high heat until lightly browned – this will take about 2–3 minutes.

■ To serve, place three slices of fried potato on each serving plate. Top each with a sautéed prawn and surround with some of the sauce. Serve immediately.

Serves 4

295 cals per portion

24 g fat per portion

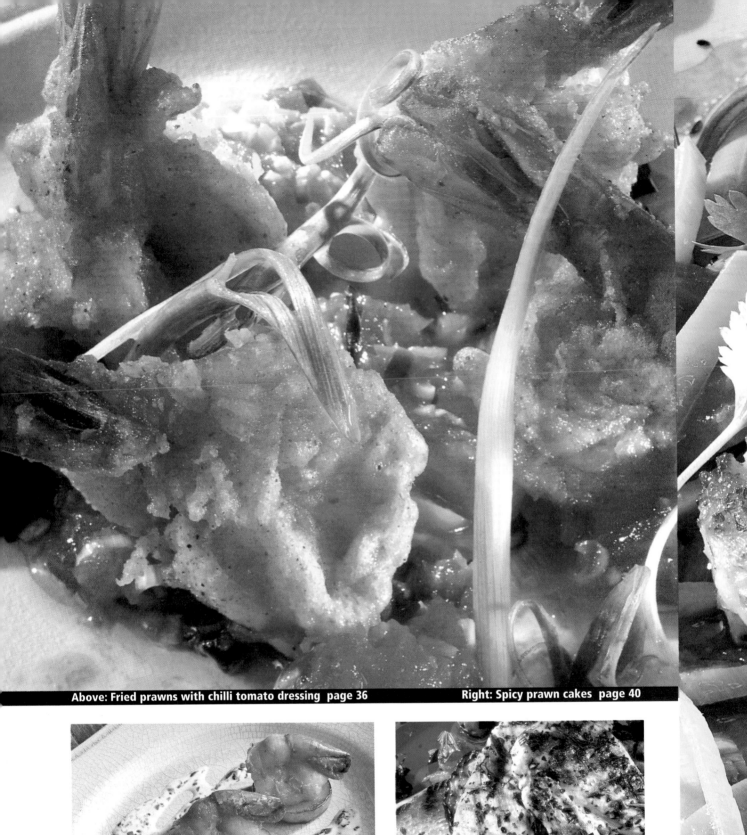
Above: Fried prawns with chilli tomato dressing page 36

Right: Spicy prawn cakes page 40

Sautéed prawns with potato and basil cream page 37

Chicken bruschetta page 41

Spicy prawn cakes with leek and ginger vinaigrette

Essentially these are Asian fish cakes, but in Asia, fish purée, chicken or pork would be used instead of mashed potato. The fish or meat gives the cakes a denser texture. Feel free to substitute salmon or cod for the prawns.

225 g (8 oz) raw prawns, peeled and
  de-veined
175 g (6 oz) cod, whiting or sole,
  skin and bones removed
1 egg
90 ml (3 fl oz) whipping cream
1 tsp ginger, chopped or grated
1 red chilli, finely chopped
3 tbsp fresh coriander, chopped
1 tbsp cornflour
1 tbsp sesame oil
½ tsp salt
2 tbsp vegetable oil for frying
Coriander sprigs to garnish

VINAIGRETTE
75 ml (2½ fl oz) vegetable oil
1 tbsp freshly grated ginger
200 g (7 oz) leeks, thinly sliced
Salt and freshly ground black pepper
3 plum tomatoes, peeled, de-seeded
  and diced
1 tbsp white wine vinegar
1 tbsp sesame oil
2 tbsp light soy sauce
2 tsp sugar

■ Roughly slice the prawns and cod, or chosen fish. Place in a food processor with the egg and whipping cream, and blend until it has a rough mince-like texture. Add the remaining ingredients, except the vegetable oil and garnish, and blend again. If the mixture seems too soft, chill in the fridge to make it firmer. Shape into 8 equal-sized patties.

■ To make the vinaigrette, heat 1 tbsp of the vegetable oil in a pan. Add the grated ginger and fry for 30 seconds. Add the leeks, 3 tbsp water and a little salt and cook over a high heat for 5 minutes. Add the plum tomatoes and freshly ground black pepper, then remove the pan from the heat. In a small bowl, whisk together the white wine vinegar, sesame oil, light soy sauce, sugar and remaining vegetable oil. Stir into the warm leek mixture.

■ To cook the prawn cakes, heat the oil over a moderate heat in a large, non-stick frying pan. Add the prawn cakes and sauté for 3–4 minutes on each side, until golden.

■ To serve, spoon some vinaigrette on to each plate and top with 2 prawn cakes. Garnish with coriander sprigs and serve immediately.

Serves 4
519 cals per portion
39 g fat per portion

Chicken bruschetta with aubergines, tomato and olives

Bruschetta is here to stay because it's just too good and versatile to give up. Learn the technique of oil-brushing, toasting and garlic-rubbing the bread, and put anything you like on top for a smart starter, snack or a light lunch.

4 skinned chicken breast fillets,
    about 100 g (3½ oz) each
100 ml (3½ fl oz) olive oil
Salt and cracked black pepper
2 tbsp chopped parsley and thyme
1 large aubergine, cut into 2 cm
    (¾ in) slices
4 long baguette slices, diagonally cut
1 clove of garlic, peeled
2 tomatoes, peeled, de-seeded and
    diced
24 black olives, stoned and roughly
    chopped
2 tbsp extra virgin olive oil
1 tbsp balsamic vinegar

■ Pre-heat the grill (or barbecue) to high. Lay each chicken breast flat on a cutting board and slice in half horizontally. Smear each chicken piece with just enough olive oil to make it glossy, then season with salt, pepper and half the herbs.

■ Brush the aubergine and bread slices with olive oil on both sides. Season the aubergine and grill for 3–4 minutes on each side until lightly browned.

■ Keep warm while you grill the chicken for 2–3 minutes on each side. Grill the bread slices until crisp and rub the cut sides twice with the garlic.

■ Season the tomatoes with a little salt, then add the olives, olive oil, vinegar, pepper and remaining herbs. Divide the aubergine slices between the baguette slices and top each with 2 pieces of grilled chicken. Spoon the tomato and olive mixture around the bruschetta and serve immediately.

Serves 4
488 cals per portion
31.15 g fat per portion

Warm falafel salad page 50

salads

Pasta salad page 48

Far left: Seared beef oriental salad
page 60

Left: Black bean, tomato and avocado salsa
page 44

Black bean, tomato and avocado salsa

We are not sure if this dish is a salad or a salsa, but it goes wonderfully with grilled meat and fish, and as the ingredients have Mexican overtones we call it a salsa. It needs to stand for at least half an hour before serving.

125 g (4 oz) black beans

1½ cloves of garlic

1½ tsp salt

3 plum tomatoes, peeled, de-seeded and cut into dice

2 avocados, peeled, stoned and diced

1 small red onion, thickly sliced

2 jalapeño chillies, sliced

4 tbsp cooked fresh or frozen sweetcorn kernels

4 tbsp lemon or lime juice

200 ml (7 fl oz) extra virgin olive oil

4 tbsp chopped fresh coriander

■ Soak the beans overnight in cold water. Drain and bring to the boil in 700 ml (1¼ pt) fresh water with a garlic clove. Cook for 20 minutes, or until soft, adding 1 tsp salt 5 minutes before the end.

■ Rinse the beans under cold water and discard the garlic. Put the beans in a large bowl. Add the tomatoes, avocado, onion, chillies, sweetcorn and the remaining finely chopped half clove of garlic and salt. Toss in the lemon or lime juice, olive oil and coriander. Leave to stand for about 30 minutes before serving.

Serves 4–6

391 cals per portion

35 g fat per portion

Tomato salad with asiago cheese

With so many types of tomato around in late summer, it's best to use as many different shapes and colours as you can find for this refreshing starter. If you can't lay your hands on Asiago cheese, use diced mozzarella or Parmesan shavings instead.

500 g (1 lb 2 oz) assorted yellow and red tomatoes of various types and sizes
Sea salt
Cracked or coarsely ground black pepper
Handful of chopped fresh basil and parsley
200 g (7 oz) Asiago cheese, crumbled

DRESSING
4 tbsp balsamic vinegar
125 ml (4 fl oz) extra virgin olive oil
2 shallots, peeled and thinly sliced into rounds
½ tsp sea salt
Crusty bread to serve

■ First make the dressing by combining all the ingredients in a small bowl. Leave to stand for 1 hour.

■ To make the salad, peel the larger tomatoes by plunging them into boiling water for 12 seconds to loosen the skins. Rinse them in cold water. Cut all the tomatoes into chunks to show off their natural shape (e.g. cut the long ones lengthways), then sprinkle them with sea salt, coarse black pepper and herbs.

■ Arrange a selection of tomatoes on each plate and scatter the crumbled Asiago cheese over the top. Spoon on the dressing and serve with fresh, crusty bread.

Serves 4–6
201 cals per portion
19 g fat per portion

Tomato salad page 45

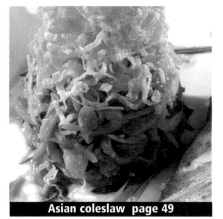
Asian coleslaw page 49

Grilled mushroom, asparagus and parmesan salad

This can be a side dish, a first course, or a light lunch if served on a bed of fresh salad greens. Cooking in a ribbed grill pan brings out the best of the vegetables, which hardly need more than a drizzle of oil, a splash of balsamic vinegar and a sprinkle of Parmesan. One of our favourites!

4 large field mushrooms or 175 g (6 oz) brown caps or oyster mushrooms
1 bunch of large asparagus spears
2 to 3 tbsp light olive oil
Salt and ground black pepper
4 tbsp extra virgin olive oil
2 tbsp balsamic vinegar
2 tbsp flat-leaf parsley, chopped
25 g (1 oz) Parmesan cheese, slivered or grated
Cracked black pepper
Flat-leaf parsley to garnish

■ Trim the stalks from the mushrooms and wipe off any excess dirt with kitchen paper. Cut the coarse stalks off the bottom of each asparagus spear if necessary. Blanch the asparagus in boiling salted water for 5 minutes or until just al dente. Rinse under cold water and drain well.

■ Heat a ridged grill pan (preferably a heavy-duty, cast-iron type) or a heavy frying pan over a high heat. Brush the mushrooms and asparagus with light olive oil and season well. Cook the mushrooms for 3 minutes on each side until tender and marked from the grill pan. Set aside and keep warm. Cook the asparagus for about 3 minutes, turning occasionally.

■ Serve straight from the pan with the mushrooms or asparagus left whole. Alternatively, thickly slice the mushrooms and cut the asparagus into angled slices and serve warm or at room temperature.

■ Divide the mushrooms and asparagus between serving plates, sprinkle with extra virgin olive oil, balsamic vinegar, parsley, Parmesan and a little cracked black pepper and garnish.

Serves 4
206 cals per portion
19 g fat per portion

Pasta salad with flageolet beans, roast peppers, rocket and chilli dressing

Here we have an age-old Italian comfort dish. Any pasta and any beans, plus vegetables for crunch and flavour, can be eaten warm as a starter – and it makes a great vegetarian main course.

225 g (8 oz) dried flageolet beans, soaked overnight in cold water

1 small onion, halved

1 small carrot

Salt

1 red pepper

1 yellow pepper

125 ml (4 fl oz) olive oil

1½ tsp dried red chillies, crushed

2 cloves of garlic, finely chopped

2 tbsp lemon juice

200 g (7 oz) large macaroni or penne pasta

1 large bunch of rocket leaves

Slivers of fresh Parmesan to garnish

★ You can cook the peppers under the grill if you prefer.

■ Pre-heat the oven to 200°C/400°F/Gas 6. Drain and rinse the beans, cover with cold water in a heavy-based pan and bring to the boil. Add the onion and carrot, and simmer gently for about 1 hour until the beans are tender but still holding their shape. About 15 minutes from the end of the cooking time, add salt. Drain the beans and discard the vegetables.

■ Rub the peppers with a little olive oil and roast in the pre-heated oven until the skins are well blistered. Cover the roasted peppers with cling-film until cool, then peel, de-seed and cut them into strips.

■ Gently heat the rest of the olive oil in a small pan with the peppers, chillies and garlic. Warm gently for 15 minutes and leave to cool. Add the lemon juice and salt to taste.

■ Meanwhile, bring a large pan of salted water to the boil and cook the pasta until al dente. Drain and rinse under cold water then drain again. In a large bowl, toss the pasta, beans, pepper strips and dressing. Add the rocket just before you serve, garnished with slivers of fresh Parmesan.

Serves 4 as a starter

574 cals per portion

25.09 g fat per portion

Asian coleslaw with crispy fried won tons

Satay ingredients in the dressing give this cabbage salad a special flavour. A tangle of deep-fried won ton or spring roll wrappers on top adds a crisp bite. Serve with fish or chicken, or as part of a cold party spread.

250 g (9 oz) white cabbage, finely shredded

1 small carrot, finely grated

2 tbsp pickled ginger, finely chopped

3–4 tbsp soy sauce, preferably Japanese

1 tbsp peanut butter

1 tbsp sugar

2 tbsp lime juice

½ tsp chilli powder (optional)

4 tbsp fresh coriander, chopped

2 tbsp spring onions, finely sliced

1 packet won ton or spring roll wrappers

Oil for deep frying

Salt

★ Won ton wrappers, pickled ginger and Japanese soy sauce can be found in Asian groceries and larger supermarkets.

■ In a ceramic bowl, combine the cabbage, carrot and ginger. Then mix together, in a separate bowl, the soy sauce, peanut butter, sugar, lime juice and, if you like a hottish flavour, the chilli powder. Add to the cabbage mixture and leave to marinate for at least 1 hour (or up to 3 hours).

■ When you are ready to serve, toss in the coriander and spring onions.

■ Heat the oil in a wok or wide pan to 180°C/350°F, separate the won ton wrappers, cut into fine strips and deep-fry in batches until crisp and golden brown. Drain on kitchen paper and sprinkle on plenty of salt. Pile on top of the coleslaw and serve at once with fish or chicken.

Serves 4–6

182 cals per portion

11.41 g fat per portion

Hummus with warm falafel and green bean salad

There's nothing like the taste of homemade hummus, and with the falafel it makes an incredibly moreish dish.

500 g (1 lb 2 oz) chickpeas, soaked in water for 24 hours

HUMMUS
½ the raw, soaked chickpeas
2 cloves of garlic, crushed
4 tbsp lemon juice
Pinch of ground cumin
½ tsp salt
4 tbsp tahini

FALAFEL
½ the raw, soaked chickpeas
1 large onion, very finely chopped
2 cloves of garlic, crushed
4 tbsp chopped parsley
4 tbsp chopped coriander
2 tsp ground cumin
½ tsp chilli powder
2 tbsp flour
½ tsp salt
Oil for deep-frying

DRESSING
150 ml (5 fl oz) extra virgin olive oil
2 tbsp lemon juice
Salt and freshly ground black pepper

SALAD
Mixed salad leaves
4 ripe tomatoes, diced
225 g (8 oz) green beans, cooked
1 medium red onion, finely diced

■ To make the hummus, boil the first amount of soaked chickpeas for 1–2 hours until tender – the timing will depend on how fresh they are.

■ Drain the chickpeas, reserving about 290 ml (½ pt) of the cooking liquid, and add them to a blender or food processor with the garlic, lemon juice, cumin, 3 tbsp of the cooking liquid, salt and tahini. Purée until smooth. If the mixture is too thick, add a little more cooking liquid.

■ To make the falafel, place the raw chickpeas in a food processor and pulse until lightly broken. Add the remaining ingredients, except the oil, and continue pulsing until you have a smooth but distinctly grainy purée. Gently form the mixture into about 40 small patties, making each roughly the size of a 50p piece.

■ Fry a few patties at a time in hot oil (170°C/325°F) for about 3–4 minutes, or until crisp and golden.

■ To serve, spoon 5 small helpings of hummus on each plate and place a falafel patty on top of each. Whisk together the olive oil, lemon juice and a little salt and pepper and drizzle 1 tbsp of the mixture over the salad leaves. Mix the tomato, beans and onion with a little more dressing, and place between the patties. Pile some salad leaves on each plate and drizzle with the remaining dressing.

Serves 8
423 cals per portion
25 g fat per portion

Crispy fried goat's cheese salad

A firm favourite in our household, and at the restaurant, there's something so tasty and appealing about a good fresh goat's cheese. If you're worried about the calories, simply omit the breadcrumb stage and grill the goat's cheese instead.

300 g (10½ oz) goat's cheese log with skin, such as Chèvre
Flour for dredging
1 egg mixed with 2 tbsp milk
Fresh breadcrumbs
Vegetable oil for frying

DRESSING
4 tbsp olive oil
4 tbsp walnut, hazelnut or vegetable oil
2 tbsp red wine vinegar
1 tsp Dijon mustard
Salt and freshly ground black pepper

SALAD
About 100 g (3½ oz) mixed salad leaves
1 small avocado, peeled and diced
2 oz (55 g) walnuts, lightly toasted and skinned
20 small black olives
Chervil leaves to garnish

■ Allow the goat's cheese to come to room temperature. Slice the log into 4 even slices. Dredge each slice in flour, then dip in the egg mixture and finally into the breadcrumbs, pressing the slices firmly into the breadcrumbs to cover each piece.

■ In a small bowl, whisk together all the dressing ingredients.

■ Heat a large frying pan over a moderate heat. Pour in enough vegetable oil to coat the bottom of the pan by 0.5 cm (¼ in). When the oil is hot, fry the goat's cheese slices for 2 minutes on each side until crisp and golden. Drain on kitchen paper.

■ Toss the salad leaves, avocado, walnuts and olives in half the dressing. Place some salad in the centre of each plate and top with the cheese slices. Spoon over a little more dressing, garnish with chervil leaves, and serve.

Serves 4
721 cals per portion
62 g fat per portion

Winter salad with roquefort and beetroot vinaigrette

Winter salad leaves have a bitterness that invites sweetness in the dressing. Here it comes from beetroot, the sweetest of roots. You can substitute other blue cheeses to finish the salad, but none has the exquisite creamy saltiness of Roquefort.

1 small head frisée lettuce

1 small head radicchio

1 bunch watercress

2 heads chicory

55 g (2 oz) walnuts, toasted

125 g (4 oz) Roquefort

VINAIGRETTE

2 cooked, peeled beetroot (55–65 g/around 2 oz) peeled weight

½ tsp salt

½ tsp freshly ground black pepper

½ tsp Dijon mustard

2–4 tbsp white wine vinegar

230 ml (7½ fl oz) light olive oil or vegetable oil

■ Trim, wash and dry all the salad leaves and mix them together.

■ To make the vinaigrette, cut the beetroot into 1 cm (½ in) dice. Mix the salt, pepper and mustard into the vinegar and, when the salt has dissolved, whisk in the oil, slowly at first to allow it to be incorporated.

■ Pour half the vinaigrette into a blender or food processor with half the beetroot and purée, then mix it back into the rest of the vinaigrette and stir in the rest of the beetroot.

■ To serve, arrange a mound of salad leaves on each plate, sprinkle the walnuts and beetroot vinaigrette around each and crumble over the Roquefort.

Serves 6

158 cals per portion

14 g fat per portion

Summer salad Roscoff with lobster and a basil mayonnaise

At Roscoff, our restaurant in Belfast, the lobsters arrive straight from the coast. If you prefer, you can use king prawns instead – allow 5 per person.

MAYONNAISE

1 tbsp Dijon mustard

Salt and freshly ground white
  pepper

1 tbsp white wine vinegar

3 egg yolks

500 ml (18 fl oz) vegetable oil or
  light olive oil

10–12 fresh basil leaves, chopped

VINAIGRETTE

½ tsp salt

½ tsp freshly ground black pepper

2 tsp Dijon mustard

3 tbsp white wine vinegar

3 tbsp balsamic vinegar

225 ml (8 fl oz) olive oil or mixed
  olive and vegetable oils

SALAD

1 lobster, about 700–750 g (1½–1¾ lb)

100 g (3½ oz) mixed salad leaves

6 red and 6 yellow cherry tomatoes,
  halved

¼ cucumber, peeled, de-seeded and
  sliced

50 g (1¾ oz) shelled broad beans,
  blanched and peeled

2 eggs, boiled for 9 minutes,
  quartered

■ To make the mayonnaise, whisk together the mustard, salt, pepper and vinegar in a bowl until the salt has dissolved. Beat in the egg yolks then add the oil, drop by drop at first then slightly faster as the mayonnaise starts to build up – always make sure each addition is worked in completely before adding more. (You'll serve only about a quarter of the mayonnaise with this salad, but it keeps for a few days covered in the fridge.)

■ To make the vinaigrette, dissolve the salt with the pepper and mustard in the vinegars in a small bowl. Whisk in the oil, slowly at first to allow it to mix in, then adjust the seasoning.

■ To cook your own lobster, tie it in a plastic carrier bag and leave it in the freezer for a couple of hours. It will then be unconscious when you put it in a large pot of vigorously boiling, generously salted water. Cook for about 14 minutes, then plunge the lobster into ice-cold water. Shell and clean it, then slice the meat neatly.

■ To serve, toss the salad leaves in vinaigrette and pile in the centre of each plate. Surround with the cherry tomatoes, cucumber, beans, eggs and lobster meat. Mix the chopped basil into the mayonnaise at the last minute so that it does not have time to discolour and spoon some on the side of each plate.

Serves 4

430 cals per portion

37.87 g fat per portion

Warm prawn salad with spiced tomato and avocado butter

A starter salad inspired by new-wave American cooking, with a sauce from France.

400 g (14 oz) raw king prawns in their shells

3 tbsp whipping cream

1 tbsp chopped shallot

2 small green chillies, de-seeded and chopped

2 cloves of garlic, chopped

1 tsp hot chilli sauce

100 g (3½ oz) unsalted butter, chilled and diced

1 tbsp lemon or lime juice

Salt and freshly ground black pepper

5 tbsp vegetable oil

2 plum tomatoes, skinned, de-seeded and roughly chopped

1 small avocado, peeled and diced

2 tbsp fresh coriander, roughly chopped

1 tbsp snipped chives (optional)

100 g (3½ oz) mixed salad leaves

2 tbsp vinaigrette

Fresh chives to garnish

★ Chilli sauce is sold under various brand names – Tabasco is probably the best known and the most widely available.

■ Shell the prawns and cut along the centre of the outer curve of each one, pulling out the thin dark thread. This opens up or 'butterflies' the prawns for a pretty effect and looks even better if you leave the tails on.

■ In a small pan, boil the cream with the shallot, chillies, garlic and chilli sauce. Turn down the heat and whisk in the butter, a cube or two at a time. Add the lemon or lime juice, season and keep warm.

■ Heat the vegetable oil in a large, heavy frying pan until almost smoking, then fry the prawns until pink and cooked. This will take about 2 minutes over a high heat.

■ Lightly season the tomato and avocado and add to the warm butter sauce. Heat until hot, but not boiling. Add the chopped coriander and chives, if using, and swirl to release the flavours.

■ Toss the salad leaves in the vinaigrette and arrange in a little pile in the centre of each serving plate. Spoon the sauce around the salad leaves and arrange the prawns on top of the sauce but not on top of the salad. Garnish with fresh chives and serve while the prawns and sauce are still warm.

Serves 4

490 cals per portion

45.16 g fat per portion

Warm chicken liver salad page 56

Warm chicken liver salad with lentils and balsamic vinaigrette

A fantastic combination of textures and tastes. The cooking time for the lentils will vary, so keep an eye on them. Soaking the livers overnight and preparing the lentils ahead makes this a quick recipe for a last-minute meal.

340 g (12 oz) chicken livers
250 ml (9 fl oz) milk
225 g (8 oz) brown or green lentils
1 small onion, finely chopped
½ carrot, finely chopped
½ celery stick, finely chopped
1 bay leaf
Pinch of dried thyme
Salt
120 ml (4 fl oz) vegetable oil
1 medium onion, finely sliced
2 tbsp butter
Salad leaves, such as oak leaf,
  lettuce and red chard
1 tbsp finely chopped chives

BALSAMIC VINAIGRETTE
50 ml (1½ fl oz) balsamic vinegar
Freshly ground black pepper
100 ml (3 fl oz) extra-virgin olive oil

■ Trim the livers, place in a bowl and cover with the milk. Leave in the fridge for at least 1 hour.

■ Wash the lentils and place in a heavy-based pan with 570 ml (1 pt) water. Bring to the boil, then reduce the heat and simmer for 5 minutes. Remove any froth that forms on the surface using a slotted spoon.

■ Add the chopped vegetables, bay leaf, thyme and 1 tsp salt and simmer for 15 minutes, or until just cooked. Remove from the heat and set aside until lukewarm.

■ Heat the oil in a frying pan, add the onion and fry until golden and crispy. Remove and drain the onion on kitchen paper. Season with salt.

■ For the vinaigrette, dissolve a little salt with the balsamic vinegar in a small bowl. Grind in some black pepper and stir in the olive oil. Drain any excess liquid from the lentils and stir in half the vinaigrette.

■ Drain and discard the milk from the liver. Pat the liver dry with kitchen paper and season. Melt the butter in a large frying pan over a high heat until foamy. Add the livers and brown on each side. Remove from the pan, reserving the juices, and keep warm.

■ To serve, spoon some of the lentil mixture around the outside of each plate. Toss the salad leaves with a little of the remaining balsamic vinaigrette and place in the centre of each plate. Top with the chicken livers, drizzle over the reserved juices and sprinkle over the fried onion and chopped chives. Serve any leftover balsamic vinaigrette separately.

Serves 4

816 cals per portion

62 g fat per portion

Caesar salad

This is the best-selling salad in our restaurant. There are many variations but we hope you like ours.

1 large cos lettuce

55g (2 oz) Parmesan, grated

20 black olives, stoned

DRESSING

Pinch of salt

1½ tsp Dijon mustard

30 ml (1 fl oz) fresh lemon juice

1 clove of garlic, crushed

2 tsp Worcestershire sauce

10 drops Tabasco

1 egg yolk

3 anchovies, crushed (a garlic press works well)

90 ml (3 fl oz) light olive oil

GARLIC CROUTONS

1 clove of garlic, peeled

6 slice of continental-style bread, crusts removed

4 tbsp olive oil

■ For the dressing, dissolve the salt and mustard in the lemon juice. Add the garlic, Worcestershire sauce, Tabasco, egg yolk and the crushed anchovies. Slowly add the oil to the mixture in a slow and steady stream, whisking continuously. Season to taste.

■ For the garlic croûtons, pre-heat the grill to medium-high. Brush both sides of each bread slice with olive oil and grill until crisp and golden. Remove from the grill and immediately rub both sides with the clove of garlic and cut into 2 cm (1 in) sq cubes.

■ Wash the lettuce and pat dry. Break the bigger outer leaves roughly, keeping the smaller inside ones whole. Toss with the dressing and two-thirds of the grated Parmesan.

■ To serve, arrange the leaves in the centre of each plate and garnish with the garlic croûtons, black olives and remaining Parmesan.

Serves 4–6

490 cals per portion

42 g fat per portion

Spicy chicken salad with basil and glass noodles

Don't let the list of ingredients in this recipe put you off – essentially it is a simple salad that can be whipped up in very little time.

450 g (1 lb) skinless chicken fillets

4 tbsp salted peanuts, roughly chopped, to garnish

MARINADE

1 tsp curry powder

1 clove of garlic, crushed and finely chopped

1 tbsp brown sugar

1 tbsp light soy sauce

1 tbsp chilli sauce

2 tbsp chopped fresh basil

2 tbsp vegetable oil

DRESSING

1 tbsp lemon juice

2 tbsp light soy sauce

1 tsp caster sugar

1 tbsp chilli sauce

4 tbsp vegetable oil

SALAD

125 g (4 oz) packet of rice vermicelli

1 small red onion, very finely sliced

1 small bunch of basil

Mixed salad leaves

1 red pepper, cut into fine strips

2 green chillies, finely sliced (optional)

■ Cut the chicken fillets into 3 cm (1¼ in) strips and place in a large bowl. Combine the marinade ingredients and pour over the chicken. Mix well, then leave to marinate for 30 minutes.

■ Pre-heat the grill to high. Place the chicken strips on a grill tray and cook for 5 minutes without turning. When cooked, remove and cover with foil.

■ To make the dressing, stir together all the ingredients in a small bowl and set aside.

■ Place the rice vermicelli in a large bowl and cover with boiling water. Leave for about 10 minutes, until soft.

■ Place the sliced onion in iced water for 2–3 minutes. This will make it crisp and mellow the flavour a little. Drain both the vermicelli and the onion, and place in a large bowl. Tear the basil leaves away from the stalks and add to the bowl, along with the salad leaves, red pepper and chillies, if using.

■ To serve, add the chicken strips, juices and dressing to the salad. Toss gently with your hands and arrange on serving plates. Scatter with the roughly chopped peanuts and serve immediately.

Serves 4

494 cals per portion

26 g fat per portion

Seared beef oriental salad

This dish mixes Japanese flavours with the classic Italian carpaccio. Try it – we think it works very well.

500 g (1 lb 2 oz) beef fillet, trimmed
½ tsp salt
1 tsp cracked black pepper
1 tbsp vegetable oil

DRESSING
60 ml (2 fl oz) Japanese soy sauce
1 tbsp sesame oil
30 ml (1 fl oz) vegetable oil

GARNISH
2 cos lettuce leaves, finely sliced
1 celery stick, sliced diagonally
2 tbsp pickled ginger
1 spring onion, finely sliced
1 tbsp black and white sesame seeds, toasted

■ Heat a heavy cast-iron frying pan over a high heat until very hot. Season the beef fillet with salt, pepper and oil, and sear in the very hot pan for 1 minute on each side, until charred on the outside but still very rare on the inside. Allow to cool.

■ Very thinly slice each fillet and place each piece between 2 sheets of oiled cling-film. Use a rolling pin to slightly flatten each piece.

■ Mix together all the dressing ingredients in a small bowl.

■ To serve, arrange 2 or 3 slices of beef on each plate and scatter over the garnish. Spoon on the dressing and serve immediately.

Serves 4
287 cals per portion
18 g fat per portion

Warm beef salad with bacon and a roquefort dressing

We prefer to use grass-fed or organic beef in our recipes. For this main-course salad, we've added Roquefort to the dressing, but Stilton or any other good blue cheese works just as well. Serve with potato skins or chips.

4 fillet steaks of beef
Salt and freshly ground black pepper
6 rashers streaky bacon, cut into strips
125 ml (4 fl oz) olive oil
3 tbsp red wine vinegar
50 g (1¾ oz) Roquefort cheese
Salt and freshly ground black pepper
100 g (3½ oz) mixed salad leaves
4 tbsp fried bread croûtons
1 avocado, stoned and diced
1 tbsp snipped chives and a few chervil leaves to garnish

■ Make sure the steaks are well trimmed and free of fat and sinew. Season with salt and pepper and allow to come to room temperature.

■ Fry the bacon in a dry pan until lightly crisp. Lift out of pan with a slotted spoon. Leave to drain on kitchen paper until it is cool enough for you to crumble with your fingers.

■ Whisk the olive oil and vinegar in a bowl, crumble in the Roquefort and mix a little to combine the flavours. Season with salt and pepper.

■ While the steaks fry to your liking in the same pan you used for the bacon, carefully arrange the salad leaves in the centre of each plate. Sprinkle the bacon and croûtons over the salad and place the avocado among the leaves.

■ When the steaks are cooked, set one right in the middle of each salad. Spoon the Roquefort dressing around and garnish with chives and chervil leaves.

Serves 4
590 cals per portion
45.67 g fat per portion

Potato ravioli with black truffle page 68

pasta &

Risotto with mushrooms and ginger page 77

risotto

Tagliatelle with roast artichokes, cherry tomatoes and basil pesto

A fresh pesto is one of the zippiest ways to use a summer surplus of fresh basil. We love to serve it simply with pasta and a few choice vegetables.

4 large globe artichokes

Juice of half a lemon

4 tbsp light olive oil

Salt

8 red cherry tomatoes, halved

8 yellow cherry tomatoes, halved

340 g (12 oz) dried tagliatelle

Freshly ground black pepper

A few basil leaves to garnish

Fresh Parmesan, finely grated

BASIL PESTO

55 g (2 oz) fresh basil leaves, roughly
  chopped

2 tbsp pine nuts

2 cloves of garlic, roughly chopped

125 ml (4 fl oz) olive oil

70 g (2½ oz) freshly grated Parmesan

Salt and freshly ground black pepper

■ To make the pesto, place all the ingredients, except the Parmesan, in a food processor and mix until it is well blended. Stir in the grated Parmesan and season to taste. Transfer to a bowl and put to one side.

■ To prepare the artichokes, carefully trim all the outer leaves from the artichokes until you are left with only the heart. Carefully cut out the hairy choke, trim off the tougher outer pieces and cut the heart into bite-sized wedges. Place the wedges in lemon juice as you work.

■ Heat a large frying pan over a medium heat. Lift the artichoke heart pieces out of the lemon juice with a slotted spoon and drain on kitchen paper. Add 2 tbsp of the olive oil to the frying pan, add the artichoke pieces, and season with a little salt. Sauté for 5 minutes, tossing occasionally until the artichoke pieces are slightly brown and can be easily pierced with a fork.

■ Turn the heat off and add the halved cherry tomatoes, cover and put to one side. (The heat of the pan and the artichokes will be enough to heat the tomatoes through without making them lose their shape and texture.)

■ Cook the tagliatelle in a large pot of boiling water to which has been added 2 tbsp salt and 2 tbsp oil. When the pasta is al dente, drain into a colander. Tip the pasta back into the pot and season with salt and freshly ground pepper. Stir in 6 tbsp of the basil pesto.

■ To serve, divide on to warm serving plates and top with the vegetables. Sprinkle over some of the fresh Parmesan and garnish with a couple of basil leaves. Serve immediately with the remaining pesto and plenty of Parmesan on the side.

Serves 4

587 cals per portion

25 g fat per portion

Tagliatelle with chicken, ham, peas and cream

This quick and tasty pasta dish is suitable for all occasions.

2 tbsp butter

1 small onion, finely chopped

1 stick of celery, finely chopped

2 cloves of garlic, finely chopped

450 g (1 lb) boneless, skinless
   chicken breasts, cut into 2.5 cm
   (1 in) cubes

Salt

250 ml (9 fl oz) chicken stock

½ tsp dried thyme

290 ml (½ pt) double cream

0.5 cm (¼ in) thick slices of cooked
   ham, cut into 2.5 cm (1 in) cubes

100 g (3½ oz) cooked or frozen peas

340 g (12 oz) dried tagliatelle

Freshly ground black pepper

2 tbsp parsley, finely chopped

4 tbsp freshly grated Parmesan

■ Melt 1 tbsp of the butter in a large saucepan. Add the onion, celery, garlic, chicken pieces, a little salt and sweat over a moderate heat for 5 minutes. Then add the chicken stock, dried thyme and cover and simmer gently for 8 minutes.

■ Add the cream, ham and peas and boil for 1 minute. Remove from the heat and, with a slotted spoon, take out the solids, place in a bowl and keep warm. Return the liquid to the boil and simmer for 5 minutes until the cream thickens slightly. Remove from the heat and return solids to the pan.

■ Meanwhile, bring a large pot of salted water to the boil. Cook the pasta until al dente, drain, season and toss with the remaining tablespoon of butter.

■ To serve, divide the pasta on to 4 warmed plates and spoon over the creamy chicken sauce. Sprinkle with parsley and Parmesan and serve immediately.

Serves 4

880 cals per portion

48 g fat per portion

Seared squid with chilli gremolata and black pasta

We love squid ink (black) pasta! Not just because of its subtle flavour but also for its mystery and relationship to the delicious squid. The gremolata oil would also go well with chicken, vegetables or roasted fish.

450 g (1 lb) squid, about 10–12.5 cm (4–5 in) long
250 g (9 oz) black tagliatelle (or other black pasta)
2 tbsp light olive oil
Salt and freshly ground black pepper
175 g (6 oz) yellow and red cherry tomatoes, halved

CHILLI GREMOLATA OIL
2 large red chillies, finely chopped
4 tbsp chopped flat-leaf parsley
1 clove of garlic, finely chopped
Grated zest of ½ lemon
1 tbsp lemon juice
120 ml (4 fl oz) extra virgin olive oil

■ To prepare the squid, separate the head and tentacles from the body and discard the stiff cartilage quill. Cut the head free from the tentacles and discard. Remove the purplish skin. Clean and rinse the squid, then cut the large tentacles in half and the body into 1 cm (½ in) ringlets.

■ To make the gremolata oil, simply stir all the ingredients together. Heat very gently, set aside and keep warm.

■ Cook the pasta in plenty of salted boiling water until al dente. Meanwhile, heat the light olive oil in a large frying pan over a high heat. When the oil is almost smoking, add the squid and season with salt and pepper. Cook for 1½–2 minutes, until the squid turns from opaque to white. Add the tomatoes and continue to cook for 30 seconds. Remove from the heat and keep warm.

■ To serve, toss the drained pasta in 2–3 tbsp of the gremolata oil. Divide the pasta between the warmed plates, then spoon over the squid and tomatoes. Drizzle with more gremolata oil and serve.

Serves 4
595 cals per portion
34 g fat per portion

Penne with mushroom pesto and asparagus

Mixing fresh with dried mushrooms adds depth of flavour, and pine nuts give an exciting texture.

1.4 kg (3 lb) asparagus
450 g (1 lb) penne
25 g (1 oz) butter
Shaved Parmesan and toasted pine
   nuts to garnish

MUSHROOM PESTO
4 tbsp light olive oil
175 g (6 oz) fresh mushrooms, sliced
15 g (½ oz) dried porcini mushrooms,
   soaked for 10 minutes in a cup of
   hot water
1 tbsp chopped garlic
55 g (2 oz) pine kernels
55 g (2 oz) grated Parmesan
4 tbsp chopped fresh parsley
Salt and freshly ground black pepper
270 ml (9 fl oz) extra virgin olive oil

■ To make the mushroom pesto, heat the olive oil in a large pan over medium high heat, add the fresh mushrooms and sauté until cooked.

■ Drain and chop the soaked porcini mushrooms and add to the fresh ones with the garlic. Cook for a further 2 minutes then empty into the bowl of a food processor. Add the remaining pesto ingredients and process to a coarse, slightly chunky purée. Season to taste with salt and freshly ground black pepper.

■ Break the fibrous ends off the asparagus and discard them. Cut the stalks at an angle and so that each piece is a little longer than the penne. Cook in a large pan of boiling, salted water. When the asparagus is just cooked, lift it out with a slotted spoon and put into a bowl of cold water. Drain, refresh under the cold tap and leave to drain in the colander.

■ Add the penne to the asparagus water, bring to the boil and cook until al dente. Return the asparagus to the pan for just 15 seconds to reheat, then drain. Return them to the pan, stir in the butter and serve in pasta bowls topped with mushroom pesto, a few shavings of Parmesan and a sprinkling of toasted pine nuts.

Serves 6
796 cals per portion
53 g fat per portion

Potato ravioli with black truffle, garlic and anchovy

The addition of black truffle makes this dish really special. Truffles are available at good speciality food stores, but can be expensive. If you can't find them, substitute with dried wild mushrooms or leave out.

8 tbsp butter
1 small onion, finely chopped
3 cloves of garlic, finely chopped
450 g (1 lb) potatoes, cut into 1 cm
  (½ in) cubes
175 ml (6 fl oz) milk
1 small black truffle, finely chopped
3 tbsp fresh parsley, finely chopped
Salt and freshly ground black
  pepper
1 quantity fresh pasta (see recipe on
  page 185)
1 egg, beaten
Flour for dusting
6 anchovy fillets, roughly chopped
Flat-leaf parsley to garnish

■ Heat 2 tbsp of the butter in a large frying pan. Add the onion and a third of the chopped garlic and sauté for about 3 minutes. Add the potatoes and milk and cover. Cook over a very low heat until tender.

■ Mash the potatoes with 2 tbsp of the butter, half the truffle, and 2 tbsp of the parsley. Season.

■ Using a pasta machine, roll the pasta very thinly to the width of the machine and about 30 cm (12 in) long. On one side of each of the strips, place small mounds of potato mixture at 7.5 cm (3 in) intervals. Brush the edges of the strips and between the potato mounds with the beaten egg, then fold the other half over the potato mounds. To seal, press along the edges and around the stuffing. Using a pastry wheel with a fluted edge, cut the ravioli into 6 cm (2½ in) squares and place each one on a tray lightly dusted with flour.

■ When ready to cook, dust off any excess flour and cook in boiling, salted water until the ravioli rises to the surface (about 2–3 minutes). Drain well and arrange on warm plates.

■ In a small saucepan, melt the remaining butter, then add the anchovy, the remaining truffle, chopped parsley and garlic, and a little pepper. Spoon the mixture over the ravioli, garnish and serve immediately.

Serves 4
698 cals per portion
36 g fat per portion

Prawns with peppers, basil and cream pasta

We do not specify the type of pasta here simply because it doesn't affect the tastiness of the dish. Be sure to get the freshest prawns – but if they aren't available, lobster would work just as well.

1 tbsp vegetable oil

340 g (12 oz) raw prawns, shelled and deveined

½ red pepper, finely sliced

½ yellow pepper, finely sliced

Salt

2 cloves of garlic, finely chopped

1 tbsp hot chilli sauce (optional)

150 ml (5 fl oz) double cream

340 g (12 oz) pasta, cooked to packet instructions

Small bunch of fresh basil leaves, shredded

Freshly ground black pepper

■ Add the oil, prawns and peppers to a large frying pan, season with a little salt and stir-fry over a high heat for about a minute. Add the garlic and fry until the prawns are cooked through.

■ Add the chilli sauce (if using) and mix well. Pour in the cream and cook until the sauce has slightly thickened, then add the pasta to warm through.

■ Remove from the heat and fold in the shredded basil. Season to taste and serve immediately.

Serves 4

567 cals per portion

23g fat per portion

Steamed won tons with chilli dipping sauce

Won tons are really Asian-style ravioli. Although easy to find in Chinese restaurants, they are never better than when you make them yourself. Won ton wrappers can be bought from Asian grocers, and freeze well.

1 packet of won ton wrappers

A few lettuce leaves

STUFFING

225 g (8 oz) chicken fillets, finely chopped or minced

225 g (8 oz) prawns, finely chopped

2 tbsp spring onions, finely chopped

1 tbsp light soy sauce

1 tbsp oyster sauce

1 tbsp dry sherry

2 tsp toasted sesame oil

1 tsp sugar

1 tsp salt

Pinch of white pepper

CHILLI DIPPING SAUCE

4 tbsp light soy sauce

2 tbsp rice wine vinegar

1 tbsp toasted sesame oil

½–1 tbsp hot chilli sauce

2 tsp minced garlic

4 tbsp spring onions, finely chopped

■ For the stuffing, mix together all the ingredients in a large bowl. Place 1 tbsp of the mixture on to the non-floured side of a won ton wrapper. Moisten the edges with water and fold up to form a little purse shape. Pinch edges together tightly to close. Continue to fill the won tons until all the stuffing is used.

■ Line a heat-proof plate with a few lettuce leaves and put the won tons on top. Place a rack in a wok or a wide pot, add 5 cm (2 in) water and bring to the boil. Put the plate with the won tons on the rack, cover and steam for 6–7 minutes or until the filling of the won tons are firm to touch. Lift the plate out and leave to cool slightly.

■ Meanwhile, mix together all the ingredients for the dipping sauce. Serve immediately with the cooked won tons on warmed plates lined with the lettuce leaves.

Serves 4–6 (makes about 25–30 won tons)

185 cals per portion

7 g fat per portion

Chicken and mushroom won tons page 72

Spiced chicken livers with chinese noodles page 73

Chicken and mushroom won tons with soy and chives

A ravioli recipe that adapts an Italian technique to include Chinese ingredients. We love it because it's so quick, and you don't even have to make pasta as won ton wrappers are sold ready-made in Chinese groceries and supermarkets.

½ medium onion, finely chopped

3 cloves of garlic, crushed

1 tsp ginger, finely chopped

175 g (6 oz) mushrooms (field, button, shitake or chestnut)

2 tbsp vegetable oil

100 g (3½ oz) raw, skinned breast of chicken

1 tbsp soy sauce

Salt and freshly ground black pepper

24 won ton wrappers

1 egg yolk, mixed with 2 tbsp cold water

SAUCE AND GARNISH

250 ml (9 fl oz) chicken stock

4 tbsp Japanese soy sauce

2 tbsp chives, snipped

A few leaves of Chinese greens, such as pak choi or choi sum, steamed

■ Cook the onion, garlic, ginger and mushrooms together in the oil in a medium-sized saucepan over medium low heat, stirring regularly, for about 10 minutes until the onions are soft and the mushrooms cooked through. Spread the mixture on a dish or baking sheet to cool quickly.

■ Purée the chicken in a food processor for about 30 seconds. Add the cooked vegetables and soy sauce, and pulse to a consistent but not too smooth mixture. Season.

■ Spread out about 4 won ton wrappers and brush lightly with the egg yolk mixture. Place 1 tsp of the filling in the centre of each wrapper and fold over to form a triangle, pressing down the edges firmly and transferring to a tray as they are finished.

■ When you are ready to eat, cook the won tons in batches for 2 minutes in a large pan of boiling, salted water.

■ To make the sauce, boil the chicken stock then add the soy sauce and chives. To serve, arrange 6 won tons on each warmed plate. Warm some steamed Chinese greens in the sauce and spoon over the cooked won tons. Serve immediately.

Serves 4

376 cals per portion

11 g fat per portion

Spiced chicken livers with chinese noodles

Although not absolutely necessary, soaking the chicken livers in milk and water makes them deliciously mild and creamy.

350 g (12 oz) fresh or frozen chicken livers
150 ml (5 fl oz) milk
1 tsp soft brown sugar
1 tsp plus 1 tbsp cracked black pepper
4 tbsp Japanese soy sauce
2 tbsp dry sherry
Salt
2 tbsp vegetable oil
1 tbsp butter
2 tsp grated fresh ginger
100 ml (3½ fl oz) double cream
2 tbsp chopped fresh coriander
1 packet of Chinese egg noodles (about 200 g/7 oz), cooked according to packet instructions
Snipped chives to garnish

■ Carefully trim the chicken livers, cutting away any bitter, greenish patches, and separate each liver into two pieces. Place the livers in a bowl and add the milk with 150 ml (5 fl oz) water. Leave in the fridge to soak for at least 1 hour.

■ Drain the chicken livers and pat dry with kitchen paper. Combine the sugar, 1 tsp cracked black pepper, soy sauce and dry sherry in a bowl. Season the livers with salt and the remaining cracked black pepper.

■ Heat the vegetable oil and butter in a large frying pan over a high heat. When the butter is foaming, add the chicken livers and fry for about 2 minutes on each side. Don't stir the livers around too much – they should be a nice brown colour. Add the ginger to the pan and fry for 30 seconds, before adding the soy sauce mixture. Allow to reduce to give the livers just a light glaze, then remove them from the pan with a slotted spoon. Set aside and keep warm.

■ Add the double cream and fresh coriander to the pan and boil until the cream thickens slightly.

■ Place the chicken livers on a pile of cooked Chinese noodles on warmed plates and pour the sauce around. Garnish and serve.

Serves 4
546 cals per portion
30 g fat per portion

Wild mushroom risotto cakes

Originally intended for using up left-over risotto, these cakes are good enough to make for their own sake.

25 g (1 oz) butter
1 medium onion, finely chopped
15 g (½ oz) dried porcini (cep)
   mushrooms, or 25 g (1 oz) dried
   Chinese black mushrooms
400 ml (14 fl oz) chicken stock
150 g (5 oz) arborio (risotto) rice
100 g (4 oz) button mushrooms,
   finely sliced
Salt and freshly ground black pepper
25 g (1 oz) fresh Parmesan, grated
3 tbsp fresh parsley, chopped
50 g (2 oz) cream cheese
Flour for dredging
1 egg, mixed with 4 tbsp milk
Fresh breadcrumbs
Oil for deep-frying
1 tsp finely chopped garlic
50 g (2 oz) butter
150 g (5 oz) mixed winter greens,
   such as cabbage, chard, spinach
100 g (4 oz) fresh wild mushrooms

■ Melt the butter in a saucepan, add the onion and sweat for 5 minutes, until soft. Meanwhile soften the dried mushrooms in a small bowl with 200 ml (7 fl oz) boiling water for 5–10 minutes, then chop coarsely. Add the soaking liquid to the stock.

■ When the onion is soft, add the rice to the pan and cook for another 2–3 minutes. Add the soaked mushrooms and button mushrooms, and cook for 3 minutes.

■ Heat the stock in a saucepan until simmering, then add two ladles of stock to the rice mixture. Adjust the heat so the added stock just simmers. Season with salt and stir frequently.

■ When the rice is almost dry, add another ladle of stock. Continue to add the stock in this way, waiting until the rice has absorbed the previous batch.

■ When the rice is cooked, season and add the Parmesan and parsley. Turn on to a baking tray and leave to cool.

■ Divide the rice mixture into 4 and roll each portion into a ball, placing a nugget of cream cheese in each. Coat the balls with flour, the egg wash and then the breadcrumbs, pressing them gently into each ball.

■ Deep-fry the risotto balls in hot oil (180°C/350°F) for 4 minutes, until golden. Drain on kitchen paper.

■ Mix the garlic and butter and place in a large saucepan with the greens and 120 ml (4 fl oz) water. Cover and bring to the boil. Simmer for 8 minutes, add the wild mushrooms, season and cook for a further 2 minutes.

■ To serve, place the greens on warmed plates and top with a risotto cake and the mushrooms.

Serves 4

667 cals per portion

44 g fat per portion

Risotto with butternut squash and sage butter

Butternut and sage complement each other wonderfully. This combination is sometimes used to fill ravioli – either way it's real comfort food.

450 g (1 lb) butternut squash
(or 450 g (1 lb) fresh pumpkin)
1.5 litres (2½ pt) chicken or vegetable
stock
Salt and freshly ground black pepper
85 g (3 oz) butter, unsalted
1 small onion, finely chopped
310 g (11 oz) arborio or other
good-quality risotto rice
55 g (2 oz) Parmesan, finely grated
1 small bunch of sage leaves,
roughly chopped

■ Peel the butternut squash and cut in half. Scoop out the seeds and cut into 2.5 cm (1 in) cubes.

■ Add the stock to a saucepan and bring to the boil, taste for seasoning and then add the squash. Cook for 10–15 minutes or until tender, then retrieve the pieces of squash with a slotted spoon. Place in another saucepan and mash roughly with a potato masher. Set aside in a warm spot.

■ Meanwhile, melt one third of the butter in a large saucepan, add the onion and cook over a gentle heat for 5 minutes. Add the rice and continue cooking for a further 2 minutes. Ladle enough stock to just cover the rice and stir.

■ Continue to add the stock, ladle by ladle, stirring continually as each one is absorbed. After about 18 minutes, or until the rice is cooked and most of the stock absorbed, stir in the Parmesan and the squash purée.

■ For the sage butter, melt the remaining butter over a high heat until it is foaming and nut-brown. Remove from the heat and add the sage.

■ To serve, place the hot risotto in warm bowls and spoon over the sage butter. Serve immediately.

Serves 4
564 cals per protion
25 g fat per portion

Risotto with mushrooms and ginger

A risotto with such distinctively Asian flavours might come as a shock if you're used to the traditional Italian recipe, but be brave and try this Oriental version. To restore the true taste of Italy to your next risotto, just leave out the ginger, substitute some Parmesan for the soy sauce and swap basil for the coriander.

40 g (1½ oz) butter
½ large onion, weighing about 150 g (5 oz), finely chopped
2 cloves of garlic, minced
½–1 tbsp chopped fresh ginger
750 ml (1¼ pt) chicken stock
8 tbsp soy sauce (preferably Japanese)
350 g (12 oz) arborio or other good-quality risotto rice
2–3 spring onions, sliced
2 tbsp chopped coriander leaves (optional)

SHITAKE MUSHROOM SAUCE
150 g (5 oz) shitake mushrooms
15 g (½ oz) butter
2 tbsp chicken stock
2 tbsp soy sauce
1 tsp sugar

■ Melt 15 g (½ oz) of the butter in a medium-sized saucepan and cook the chopped onion, garlic and ginger over a moderate heat for about 10 minutes, stirring regularly. Meanwhile, bring the chicken stock to the boil and add the soy sauce.

■ When the onion is soft, add the rice and cook, stirring frequently for 3 minutes, then add a few ladles of the hot stock, stirring all the time.

■ Add another ladle of stock as the last one is absorbed – you should always just be able to see liquid at the top. Continue stirring and adding hot stock until the rice is cooked but still a little bit firm.

■ While the rice is cooking, trim the tough stems off the mushrooms and cut the caps into thick slices. Melt 15 g (½ oz) of the butter in a saucepan over medium heat with 2 tbsp each of chicken stock and soy sauce, and the sugar. Add the sliced mushrooms and simmer gently for 2 minutes – but don't forget to stir the rice regularly as this gives the risotto its delicious creamy texture.

■ When the rice is cooked, stir in the remaining butter, along with the spring onions and fresh coriander. Ladle generously into warm bowls and top with a few tablespoons of the shitake mushrooms in their sauce.

Serves 4
565 cals per portion
13 g fat per portion

Escalope of salmon page 80

fish

Sautéed fillet of salmon page 84

Crispy fried skate page 96

& seafood

Escalope of salmon with leeks and sun-dried tomato butter

This butter is what is known as a compound butter. It can be made in advance and kept in the freezer, and goes well with most grilled meat and fish, not to mention vegetables.

400 g (14 oz) thick salmon fillet

2 medium leeks

250 g (9 oz) unsalted butter, softened

¼ tsp salt

1 tbsp snipped chives

Salt and freshly ground black pepper

1 tbsp vegetable oil

Fresh chives and coriander sprigs to garnish

SUN-DRIED TOMATO BUTTER

2 shallots, finely sliced

100 ml (3½ fl oz) dry white wine

20 sun-dried tomato halves, drained of oil

2 tbsp hot chilli sauce (optional)

Small bunch of coriander leaves, roughly chopped (about 5 tbsp)

1 tbsp snipped chives

Pinch of white pepper

■ To make the sun-dried tomato butter, put the shallots and wine in a small pan. Bring to the boil over a medium heat until the wine has almost evaporated. Roughly chop the sun-dried tomatoes and blend in a food processor with the shallot mixture, chilli sauce, coriander, chives and pepper until fairly smooth and well mixed.

■ Lay out 2 A4 size pieces of cling-film and divide the sun-dried tomato butter evenly between them. Pat each piece into a cylinder shape and carefully roll up in the cling-film. Freeze one of the packets for another time, and place the second in the fridge to chill slightly.

■ Discard any bones from the salmon fillet, removing them with a clean pair of tweezers. Cut into 4 equal portions.

■ Trim the leeks of any wilted leaves. Halve each leek lengthways, leaving it still attached at the roots. Wash under cold running water, shake dry and slice each thinly.

■ In a large saucepan over a high heat, heat the leeks with the butter, 2–3 tbsp water and a little salt. Cook very quickly for 3–4 minutes until the leeks are just tender and most of the water has evaporated. Add the snipped chives, and keep in a warm place.

■ Season the salmon pieces. Heat a large frying pan over a high heat, and add the oil to the pan, then the salmon pieces. Allow each piece to cook quickly, without moving them too much. After 3 minutes, turn the salmon pieces over and continue to cook for 2–3 minutes. The cooking time will depend on how thick the fillets are, and whether you prefer your salmon slightly pink in the middle.

■ To serve, place a bed of leeks on each warmed plate and top with a salmon fillet. Spoon some of the sun-dried tomato butter over the top, and garnish with chives and coriander sprigs.

Serves 4

584 cals per portion

53 g fat per portion

Grilled salmon with cumin, lemon and black pepper

Cumin gives this fast, colourful main course an earthy depth, while pepper and lemon lift it. We've served it here with sun-dried tomato vinaigrette and, for contrast and texture, crispy fried vegetables (see page 184) works well as an accompanying dish.

Salt

4 fresh salmon fillets, skinned and boned, each about 175 g (6 oz)

1½ tsp freshly ground black pepper

1½ tsp ground cumin

100 ml (3½ fl oz) olive oil

Zest of 2 lemons

3 tbsp lemon juice

1 clove of garlic, chopped

2 tbsp chopped parsley

SUN-DRIED TOMATO VINAIGRETTE

6 sun-dried tomatoes in oil – about 50 g (2 oz), roughly chopped

150 ml (5 fl oz) olive oil

1 tsp lemon juice

½ tsp chilli powder (optional)

■ Lightly salt the salmon fillets and spread in a dish in a single layer. Mix the pepper, cumin, olive oil, lemon zest and juice, garlic and parsley, and pour over the salmon. Marinate for 1 hour.

■ To make the sun-dried tomato vinaigrette, put all the ingredients in a food processor and blend for about 1 minute to a fairly smooth consistency. Salt may not be necessary.

■ Pre-heat the grill to high and grill the salmon fillets for 3–4 minutes on each side. Transfer to warm plates and pour the dressing over. Serve with crispy fried vegetables.

Serves 4

806 cals per portion

73 g fat per portion

Crusty salmon and chilli vegetable ragout

The colours in this dish look stunning, and it's versatile too – try replacing the salmon with cod and the cauliflower with broccoli. Serve with Coconut Rice (see page 138).

600 g (1 lb 5 oz) boneless salmon fillet, skinned and cut diagonally
Salt and freshly ground black pepper

CHILLI VEGETABLE RAGOUT
1 small cauliflower
¼ Chinese cabbage
6 spring onions, cut into 3 cm (1¼ in) lengths
4 tbsp coconut oil or vegetable oil
1 red pepper, deseeded and sliced into 0.5 cm (¼ in) strips
2 fresh chillies, deseeded and sliced into rings
3 cloves of garlic, finely chopped
4 cm (1½ in) piece of root ginger, finely sliced and cut into shreds
1 tbsp dark soy sauce
2 tbsp fish sauce
2 tbsp kecap manis (sweet Indonesian soy sauce)

■ Discard any bones from the salmon pieces, and season with salt and freshly ground black pepper.

■ For the chilli vegetable ragout, cut the cauliflower into small florets and the cabbage into rough chunks. Cook the cauliflower in salted boiling water for about 4 minutes until al dente, adding the cabbage to the pan for the last 15 seconds. Drain well and refresh in plenty of cold water. Drain again and place in a bowl with the spring onions.

■ Place 2 tbsp of the oil in a large pan over a high heat. When the oil is very hot, add the salmon and fry for 2–3 minutes on each side.

■ Meanwhile, heat the remaining oil in a large frying pan or wok. Add the pepper, chillies, garlic and ginger and sauté over a high heat for 30 seconds.

■ Add the cauliflower and cabbage and cook for a further 2 minutes until thoroughly heated through. Add the soy sauce, fish sauce and kecap manis and about 2 tbsp water. Continue to cook for another 30 seconds, or until the juices thicken slightly.

■ To serve, spoon the vegetable ragout on to each plate with a little sauce. Top with the salmon fillets and more of the vegetables, and serve immediately.

Serves 4
439 cals per portion
30 g fat per portion

Sautéed fillet of salmon with potato and chive sauce

The inspiration behind the sauce is traditional Irish 'champ' – creamy mashed potatoes with chopped spring onions. This recipe refines the formula with chives and softens it to sauce consistency with cream.

200 g (7 oz) potato (about 1 large potato), cut into 3 cm (generous 1 in) dice
½ small onion, chopped
175–200 ml (6–7 fl oz) whipping cream
Salt and freshly ground black pepper
1 tbsp cooking oil
4 x 100 g (3½ oz) skinless salmon fillets
2–3 tbsp snipped chives
A few baby spinach leaves, lightly dressed with vinaigrette (optional), and fresh chives to garnish

■ Cover the potato and onion with cold, salted water in a small saucepan, then bring to the boil over a medium heat and simmer until the potato is very soft.

■ Drain off the liquid, add the cream to the potato and bring to the boil. Take off the heat and purée in a food processor or with a potato masher. Season and keep warm.

■ Heat a large frying pan over a high heat, add the oil and tilt to coat the pan. Season the salmon fillets with salt and pepper. Fry quickly for about 2 minutes each side.

■ Add the chives to the potato purée and spoon generously on to each serving plate. Put a salmon fillet on top, garnish with spinach leaves and fresh chives and serve.

Serves 4
436 cals per portion
35 g fat per portion

Fillet of salmon with a mustard crust

The sharpness of the mustard here contrasts wonderfully with the salmon.

600 g (1 lb 5 oz) salmon fillet (about ½ to ⅔ of a side), skinned and boned
2 tbsp butter
2 tbsp vegetable oil
Dill sprigs to garnish

SAUCE
2 shallots, finely chopped
2 tbsp butter
210 ml (7 fl oz) dry white wine
75 ml (2½ fl oz) double cream
150 g (5 oz) unsalted butter, cold and diced
1 tbsp wholegrain mustard
½ tbsp chopped fresh dill

MUSTARD CRUST
100 g (3½ oz) coarse breadcrumbs
2 tbsp chopped fresh dill
Salt and freshly ground white pepper
Flour for dredging
2 tbsp wholegrain Dijon mustard

■ Pre-heat the oven to 180°C/350°F/Gas 4. Cut the salmon fillet into 4 portions, each weighing about 150 g (5 oz). Check for any bones.

■ To make the sauce, place the shallots in a medium-sized pan with the butter. Cook over a medium heat for 2–3 minutes until the shallots are soft and transparent.

■ Add the wine to the pan and boil until there is only about 4 tbsp of liquid left. Add the cream and return to the boil. After 1–2 minutes, reduce the heat to low and whisk in the butter, cube by cube. Remove from the heat and whisk in the mustard and dill. Set aside and keep warm.

■ For the mustard crust, place the breadcrumbs on a plate and mix in the chopped dill. Season the salmon portions generously with salt and white pepper then dredge lightly in the flour. Spread the top of each fillet with mustard, then press the breadcrumbs evenly over the top.

■ To cook the salmon fillets, heat the butter and oil in a frying pan over a medium high heat. When the butter foams, place the fillets in the pan, crust-side down. Cook for about 4 minutes, then transfer to a grill pan. Finish under a pre-heated grill for about 5 minutes. Alternatively, dot the fillets with butter and cook under a pre-heated grill, crust-side up, until crisp and golden. Garnish and serve with Vegetable Medley (see page 133).

Serves 4
94 cals per portion
77 g fat per portion

Baked cod with wilted tomatoes and spring onions

The secret behind the flavour of this dish is in the way it's cooked. As the fish is baked with the tomatoes, the juices intermingle to create a very tasty sauce.

8 spring onions
125 g (4 oz) cold unsalted butter, roughly diced
6 plum tomatoes, peeled, de-seeded and roughly chopped
60 ml (2 fl oz) white wine
4 thick cod fillets (with skin), each weighing 175 g (6 oz)
Salt and freshly ground black pepper

■ Pre-heat the oven to 220°C/425°F/Gas 7. Finely slice the spring onions diagonally, separating the white parts from the green. Melt 1 tbsp butter in an ovenproof dish, add the white spring onion parts and cook for 1 minute over a moderate heat, stirring constantly. Add the tomatoes and wine and continue to cook for 1 minute.

■ Season the cod fillets, leaving on the skin as it keeps the fish intact and moist during cooking, and place them on top of the tomatoes. Cover with foil and bake in the oven for 6 minutes, or until just cooked.

■ Lift the cod fillets out of the dish with a spatula and place on a warmed serving dish. Cover with foil to keep them hot while making the sauce.

■ Place the ovenproof dish over a moderate heat, add the green spring onion tops and boil vigorously to reduce the cooking liquid to about 3 tbsp. Add the remaining butter and stir quickly with a wooden spoon until well incorporated. Season to taste.

■ To serve, place a ladle of sauce and tomatoes on each plate. Top with a piece of cod, skin side up. Roll back the skin and discard it seconds before serving.

Serves 4
397 cals per portion
27 g fat per portion

Sesame fried cod with a soy mustard vinaigrette

This is a great dish with thick fillets of fresh fish sprinkled with sesame seeds and seared to a crisp crust, served with a golden mustard dressing.

Salt and freshly ground black pepper
4 thick cod fillets, each weighing
   about 150 g (5 oz), skinned
1 tbsp white sesame seeds
1 tbsp black sesame seeds
1 tbsp vegetable oil
25 g (1 oz) butter
Chives to garnish

DRESSING
2 tbsp grain mustard
1 tsp English mustard
2 tbsp caster sugar
2 tbsp rice wine vinegar
2 tbsp Japanese soy sauce
5 tbsp vegetable oil

■ Season the cod fillets and sprinkle the top with the sesame seeds, pressing them firmly into the fish. Heat a large frying pan over moderately high heat, add the oil and butter and, when the butter is foaming, put in the fish fillets, sesame-seed side down. Fry for about 5 minutes, turn carefully and cook for a further 3 minutes.

■ To make the dressing, whisk together both the mustards and the sugar with the wine vinegar and soy sauce until the sugar is dissolved, then whisk in the oil.

■ To serve, place the cod on plates and serve with Asian Coleslaw (see page 49) or sautéed cabbage (see page 184). Surround with dressing, garnish and serve.

Serves 4
385 cals per portion
27.77 g fat per portion

Grilled mackerel with roast pimentos and salsa verde

This dish is great for the barbecue but, if you prefer, you can cook it under the grill. If you're unable to find pimentos, then use conventional red peppers instead.

4 pimentos or 2 red peppers

4 tbsp light olive oil

8 unskinned mackerel fillets, about 600 g (1 lb 5 oz) in total

Salt and freshly ground black pepper

SALSA VERDE

3 tbsp chopped parsley

3 tbsp capers

4 anchovy fillets

1 clove of garlic

1 tsp Dijon mustard

1 tbsp lemon juice

100 ml (3½ fl oz) extra virgin olive oil

Flat-leaf parsley sprigs to garnish

New potatoes and green salad to serve

■ Pre-heat the grill or barbecue. Rub the pimentos or red peppers with a little light olive oil then grill or roast them on the barbecue until blistered and blackened. Cool, peel and de-seed. If you have managed to find pimentos, take care to preserve their beautiful shape: leave the stalk on, slit the flesh open and scoop out the seeds with a teaspoon. Bell peppers are best served de-seeded and halved lengthways.

■ Remove any bones from the fish using tweezers and trim the fillets into a nice neat shape. Season with salt and pepper and rub with a little olive oil. Put the fillets skin side up on a baking tray under the hot grill and cook for 5–6 minutes until the skin is crisp. If you are cooking the fillets on the barbecue, place them skin side down.

■ While the fish cooks, make the salsa verde. Grind the parsley, capers, anchovies and garlic in a food processor, or with a pestle in a mortar. When this forms a paste, add the mustard and beat in the lemon juice and extra virgin olive oil. Season with black pepper, but check before adding salt.

■ Lay 2 mackerel fillets in the centre of 4 warmed plates with a whole roast pimento – or half a red pepper – and a spoonful or two of salsa verde. Garnish the fillets with flat-leaf parsley sprigs. Serve with boiled new potatoes and salad.

Serves 4

688 cals per portion

55.33 g fat per portion

Baked monkfish with chinese black beans page 92

Grilled monkfish with chilli butter page 93

Grilled tuna niçoise

As fresh tuna is so easy to get hold of, we have been playing around a bit with the concept of the summer favourite, the salad niçoise.

800 g (1¾ lb) tuna fillets

1 tbsp cracked black peppercorns

Salt

2 tbsp light olive oil

1 yellow pepper

½ tbsp vegetable oil

2 plum tomatoes

8–12 new potatoes, cooked

175 g (6 oz) cooked French beans

Salt and freshly ground black pepper

2 tbsp extra virgin olive oil

20 olives, stoned

1 tbsp chopped fresh parsley

Flat-leaf parsley to garnish

DRESSING

¼ tsp salt

1½ tsp Dijon mustard

4 tsp lemon juice

1 clove of garlic, crushed

5 drops of Tabasco sauce

4 anchovy fillets

100 ml (3½ fl oz) light olive oil

1 raw egg yolk

■ Discard the skin and dark flesh from the fish and cut into four steaks. Season with black pepper and a little salt, pressing down firmly with your hand. Lightly coat with olive oil and chill the steaks until you are ready to cook them.

■ Rub the yellow pepper with a little vegetable oil and grill or roast until the skin is well blistered. Leave to cool, then peel off the charred skin. Remove the seeds. Slice into 8 pieces and place in a bowl. Cut each tomato into 6 wedges, slice the potatoes, if they are large, and add to the yellow pepper along with the beans. Lightly season, then toss together with the extra virgin olive oil, olives and parsley. Leave to stand at room temperature.

■ To make the dressing, put all the ingredients into a food processor and blend until smooth.

■ To cook the tuna, heat a large frying pan (preferably cast iron) over a high heat until almost smoking and sear the steaks for about 2 minutes on each side.

■ Divide the vegetables between the plates and place a tuna steak in the centre of each. Pour over the dressing, garnish and serve immediately.

Serves 4

522 cals per portion

35 g fat per portion

Baked monkfish with chinese black beans

Fermented Chinese soy beans can be an acquired taste. However, once tasted, you're addicted! They are available at Chinese groceries and large supermarkets. If you can't find the beans, substitute them with Amoy Black Bean Sauce.

4 cloves of garlic, finely chopped

2 tbsp Chinese black beans, washed and drained

1 tsp roughly chopped fresh ginger

700 g (1½ lb) boneless monkfish fillets, trimmed

1 large carrot and a few fresh coriander sprigs to garnish

MARINADE

2 tbsp light soy sauce

2 tbsp dry sherry

1 tsp sesame oil

1 tsp wine vinegar

1 tsp caster sugar

Salt and white pepper

SCALLION OIL

6 tbsp peanut oil

4 spring onions (scallions), finely sliced

2 tbsp roughly chopped coriander

■ Pre-heat the oven to 200°C/400°F/Gas 6. Place the garlic, black beans and ginger in a ceramic baking dish.

■ Cut the monkfish into 4 equal-sized fillets. Combine all the marinade ingredients in a bowl, add the monkfish and set aside for 5 minutes.

■ Arrange the monkfish fillets on top of ingredients in the dish. Spoon over the marinade juices and cover tightly with foil. Bake for 10–12 minutes, until the fish is white and firm, then remove from the oven and leave to rest for 5 minutes.

■ Meanwhile, make the scallion oil: heat the peanut oil over a moderate heat, add the spring onions and coriander and fry for 15 seconds. Pour into a heatproof dish or small saucepan and set aside.

■ To serve, place the fish fillets side by side on a warm serving dish. Spoon the garlic, black beans and juices from the baking dish over the top. Drizzle with the scallion oil.

■ For the garnish, slice the carrot lengthways into fine ribbons using a potato peeler. Blanch in lightly salted boiling water for 30 seconds, then curl into ribbons. Arrange carrot curls and coriander sprigs on the fish and serve with steamed rice (see page 185) and bok choy.

Serves 4

323 cals per portion

20 g fat per portion

Grilled monkfish with chilli butter

You will have more than enough chilli butter for 4, but it keeps well in the fridge and is excellent with other white fish or salmon. It's also good with steamed vegetables.

**450 g (1 lb) monkfish fillet, any dark
  flesh trimmed off**
Salt and freshly ground black pepper
A little butter for greasing
**Steamed bok choy (from large
  supermarkets), to serve**

CHILLI BUTTER
150 ml (5 fl oz) dry white wine
2 heaped tbsp chopped shallots
1 tbsp finely chopped garlic
2 tbsp chopped fresh basil leaves
1–2 dried chillies, crushed
1 tbsp sweet chilli sauce
1 tbsp fresh lime juice
½ tsp salt
125 g (4 oz) butter

■ Cut the monkfish into 4 portions. Slit each portion almost through horizontally and then, opening it up like a book, press it gently with the heel of your hand to flatten.

■ To make the chilli butter, boil the wine with the shallots in a small pan over a medium high heat to reduce the wine by half. Add the other ingredients except the butter then, off the heat, whisk the chilli mixture into the butter.

■ Heat the grill to high and lightly butter a large baking sheet. Season the monkfish lightly with salt and pepper and arrange on the baking sheet. Spread each portion with 1 tbsp chilli butter and grill for about 10 minutes until lightly browned.

■ Place the fish on warm serving plates with the cooking juices, plus extra chilli butter if needed. Serve at once with steamed bok choy.

Serves 4
344 cals per portion
17 g fat per portion

Medley of seafood with herbs and garlic

Fresh seafood works best for this simple and delicious dish – use a combination or even just one type. Serve as a starter or as a main course with saffron rice or pasta.

560 g (1¼ lb) seafood (eg cod, hake, salmon, prawns, mussels, oysters)
40 g (1½ oz) butter
1 tbsp chopped garlic
4 tbsp finely chopped spring onions
120 ml (4 fl oz) dry white wine
1 tsp lemon zest
400 g (14 oz) can of chopped tomatoes
A few drops of Tabasco or chilli sauce
1 tbsp chopped parsley
1 tbsp chopped chives
1 tbsp chopped chervil
A few sprigs of various herbs to garnish

■ Wash the fish and cut into 5 cm (2 in) pieces. Wash the prawns, mussels and oysters.

■ Melt half the butter in a large frying pan, add the garlic and fry until it begins to colour.

■ Add the seafood, spring onions, white wine and lemon zest. Cover and simmer for 2 minutes, then remove the lid. The oysters will have opened by now, so remove them from their shells, reserving some half-shells for serving. Return the oyster meat to the pan. Add the tomatoes and their juices, Tabasco and herbs. Simmer for 2 minutes. Turn off the heat and stir in the remaining butter.

■ Sit the oysters in their shells and serve immediately in warm bowls with the rest of the seafood. Garnish with a few sprigs of herbs.

Serves 4
223 cals per portion
10 g fat per portion

Crispy fried skate with sesame ginger vinaigrette

To prepare the vegetables for the accompanying root salad, use a mandolin or simply shave off strips with a vegetable peeler, then shred into julienne strips with a knife.

560 g (1¼ lb) fresh skate, skinned and filleted

1 egg white

1 tbsp cream

Oil for deep-frying

VINAIGRETTE

15 g (½ oz) fresh root ginger, grated and finely chopped

2 tbsp wine vinegar

1 tbsp mushroom soy sauce, or dark soy sauce

1 tbsp chilli sauce

½ bunch fresh coriander, chopped

90 ml (3 fl oz) vegetable oil

50 ml (1½ fl oz) sesame oil

Salt and ground white pepper

SPICED FLOUR

150 g (5½ oz) plain flour

1½ tsp salt

2 tsp ground white pepper

3 tbsp sesame seeds, half black and half white if possible

2 tsp chilli powder

2 tsp curry powder

ORIENTAL RADISH SALAD

1 medium carrot, cut into thin strips

½ red onion, finely sliced and soaked in iced water for 30 minutes

¼ mouli, cut into thin strips

1 bunch radish, thinly sliced

1 bunch watercress

2 tbsp soy sauce

■ To make the sesame vinaigrette, combine all the ingredients, except the oils and seasoning, in a bowl. Mix well, then slowly whisk in the oils. Season to taste and set aside.

■ Cut the skate into 5 cm (2 in) pieces. Combine the egg white and cream in a bowl, then add the fish, rubbing the mixture into it well.

■ Mix the spiced flour ingredients in a bowl, then coat the fish pieces in the mixture. Heat the oil to 180°C/350°F, and deep-fry the fish for about 2 minutes or until golden.

■ Meanwhile, prepare the salad by combining all the ingredients, except the soy sauce, with a little sesame vinaigrette. To serve, place the salad in the centre of each plate. Drain the skate on a kitchen towel and arrange on top of the salad. Surround with a little sesame vinaigrette dotted with soy sauce and serve immediately.

Serves 6

408 calories per portion

33 g fat per portion

Smoked haddock hash with poached eggs

This is a perfect dish for a lazy Sunday lunch. It's filling, satisfying and easy to prepare.

3 tbsp wine vinegar
Salt
750 g (1½ lb) smoked haddock fillet
55 g (2 oz) butter
1 medium leek, trimmed and sliced
½ yellow pepper, diced
½ red pepper, diced
4 spring onions, finely sliced
500 g (1 lb 2 oz) potatoes, peeled
   and cut in 2 cm (about 1 in) dice
2 tbsp light olive oil
2 tbsp chopped parsley
200 g (7 oz) mayonnaise
2–3 tbsp wholegrain Dijon mustard
6–8 very fresh eggs

■ Bring 2 litres (3½ pt) water to the boil, add the vinegar and 1 tbsp salt, reduce to a simmer and poach the haddock in it for 8–10 minutes, then drain. When the fish is cool enough, flake into 2 cm (about 1 in) pieces.

■ Melt half the butter in a large pan with 2 tbsp water. Add the leek, peppers and spring onions and a little salt. Cook over moderate heat for about 5 minutes, until the liquid has evaporated and the vegetables are just starting to brown. Set aside.

■ In a large pan, fry the potatoes in olive oil until golden. Gently mix in the fish, vegetables and herbs, then press down evenly with a spatula. Dot with the remaining butter, cover and cook gently for 5–7 minutes.

■ Mix the mayonnaise and mustard together.

■ Lightly poach the eggs in a wide pan of simmering water.

■ To serve, turn the hash out on to a large plate or spoon on to separate plates. Top each serving with a poached egg and serve with the mustard mayonnaise.

Serves 6–8
598 cals per portion
44 g fat per portion

Moroccan spiced lamb kebabs page 104

meat,

Braised duck legs with red wine page 124

Chargrilled breast of duck page 121

poultry
& game

Noisettes of lamb with a mustard and basil cream

A neat little joint that requires no carving – simply slice it into medallions and serve with a sumptuous creamy sauce.

**600 g (1 lb 5 oz) boned and rolled
    loin of lamb**
Salt and freshly ground black pepper
2 tbsp vegetable oil
4 tbsp white wine, stock or water
200 ml (7 fl oz) double cream
2 tbsp finely sliced basil
1–2 tbsp good-quality Dijon mustard
A little sautéed spinach to garnish

■ Season the lamb generously with salt and pepper, pressing the seasoning on to the surface. In a heavy frying pan, heat the oil until it is nearly smoking. Add the lamb and cook over high heat until well browned all round. This should take about 10 minutes, by which time the lamb will be cooked medium rare.

■ Transfer the lamb to a warm plate and cover with foil. Pour off the fat from the pan and add the wine, stock or water. Scrape in the caramelized meat juices from the bottom of the pan as the liquid comes to the boil.

■ Add the cream, bring to a fast boil, then remove from the heat and stir in the basil and mustard. To serve, slice the lamb, mixing any juices into the sauce, arrange the slices on warmed plates with a little sautéed spinach (see page 184) and spoon the sauce around it.

Serves 4
545 cals per portion
45 g fat per portion

Braised lamb shanks, with thyme, roast carrots and onions

Lamb shanks are one of the most satisfying pieces of meat both to cook and to eat. They can either be cut from the shoulder, or for a more meatier cut, taken from the leg.

4 lamb shanks
2 tbsp light olive oil
200 g (7 oz) carrots, peeled and cut
  into 2.5 cm (1 in) chunks
12 baby onions, peeled
3 fresh thyme sprigs
Salt and freshly ground black pepper
2 tbsp butter
1 tbsp flat-leaf parsley, chopped
1 tsp thyme leaves, chopped
Fresh thyme sprigs to garnish

■ Pre-heat the oven to 150°C/300°F/Gas 2. Trim any excess fat from the lamb shanks and saw off the knuckle (your butcher can do this). Heat the oil in a large, heavy casserole dish and brown the shanks on all sides. Remove the shanks, then brown the carrots and onions.

■ When the vegetables are golden brown, remove and reserve. Put the shanks and any juices back into the casserole dish with the thyme and 2 tbsp water. Season with a little salt. Cover and cook the shanks for 1½–1¾ hours, turning occasionally. Return the carrots and onions to the dish and continue to cook for 1 hour.

■ Strain off the cooking juices into a small saucepan. Using a ladle or spoon, remove any visible fat from the top of the juices. Boil the liquid for about 7 minutes until it has a light sauce consistency. Remove from the heat and stir in the butter and herbs. Season to taste.

■ Lightly season the shanks with salt and arrange on a warmed plate. Surround with the vegetables, coat with the sauce and garnish with fresh thyme. Serve with Saffron and Barley Risotto (see page 139), or mashed potatoes.

Serves 4

622 cals per portion
50 g fat per portion

Braised lamb shanks page 101

Noisettes of lamb page 100

Slow roast shoulder of lamb with rosemary

Chunky steaks cut from the shoulder marinate to tenderness overnight, to be slowly baked in wine that reduces to a rich and sticky glaze around the meat. The flavours linger in the meat from the dry marinade, but none of the ingredients appear in the finished dish, so it's important not to crush or chop the garlic, but simply to crack the peeled cloves open by tapping them with a pestle or the end of a rolling pin.

1 boned shoulder of lamb, about 1.25 kg (2¾ lb) boned weight

Salt and freshly ground black pepper

2 tbsp light olive oil

½ onion, finely chopped

1 small carrot, chopped

½ stick celery, chopped

120 ml (4 fl oz) red wine

15 g (½ oz) butter

1 tbsp chopped fresh rosemary

MARINADE

4 cloves of garlic, peeled and cracked open

4 sprigs fresh rosemary

3 tbsp light olive oil

■ Trim excess fat from the lamb and cut the meat into chunky portions of about 200 g (7 oz) each. Mix the marinade ingredients in a bowl, rub into the lamb and leave in the refrigerator overnight.

■ Pre-heat the oven to 140°C/275°F/Gas 1. Lift out the lamb, wiping off solids from the marinade, and season the pieces with salt and pepper.

■ Heat 2 tbsp oil in a large casserole until almost smoking and fry the meat until well browned. Pour off any excess fat in the pan, add the onion, carrot, celery and red wine. Cover and cook in the oven for 1 hour. Remove the lid and continue cooking, turning the meat frequently, until the meat is tender and the juices reduced to a rich glaze on the meat.

■ Lift out the lamb and keep warm. Add a splash of water to the cooking juices in the pan and strain through a fine sieve into a small pot. Add the butter and chopped rosemary and taste for seasoning. Serve on warm plates with a little of the sauce spooned over.

Serves 6

598 cals per portion

49 g fat per portion

Moroccan spiced lamb kebabs with a saffron aïoli

Spring is the best time of year to eat shoulder of lamb. It can be roasted whole, boned or chopped.

750 g (1 lb 10 oz) shoulder of lamb, boned and trimmed of excess skin and fat

SPICE MARINADE
¼ tsp garlic powder
1½ tsp cumin
¾ tsp ground coriander seeds
1½ tsp oregano
¾ tsp chilli powder or ½ tsp harissa paste
1½ tbsp freshly ground black pepper
150 ml (5 fl oz) natural yoghurt
4 bamboo skewers, soaked in cold water for 30 minutes
Salt
1 tbsp chopped parsley
1 tbsp chopped mint
1 lemon, cut into wedges, and sprigs of flat-leaf parsley to garnish

■ Cut the lamb into 3 cm (1¼ in) cubes. Mix the spices with the yoghurt and toss with the lamb pieces. Leave to marinate for at least 1 hour, although 4–6 hours or overnight is best.

■ Pre-heat the grill or barbecue to high. Thread the pieces of meat on to the bamboo skewers and season with salt. Place under the grill or on the barbecue and cook, turning occasionally, until the meat is well browned and crusted.

■ Sprinkle with herbs and drizzle with aïoli (see recipe below). Garnish with a lemon wedge and a sprig of flat-leaf parsley. Sautéed Potatoes with Prunes and Apples would also make an ideal accompaniment (see page 132).

Serves 4
420 cals per portion
41 g fat per portion

Saffron Aïoli The harissa or chilli gives this an extra kick.

125 ml (4 fl oz) chicken stock
½ tsp saffron threads
½ tsp salt
2 egg yolks
1 slice white bread, crusts removed and diced
3 tsp finely sliced garlic
1 tsp harissa paste or ¾ tsp chilli powder
300 ml (10 fl oz) light olive oil

■ Place the chicken stock in a small saucepan with the saffron threads and salt. Boil until the liquid is reduced by about a half. Pour into a food processor or liquidiser, ensuring that all the saffron goes in.

■ Add the yolks, bread, garlic and harissa paste and, with the food processor running, slowly add the oil in a steady stream. Season to taste.

Navarin of pork with rosemary and juniper

We've borrowed the term 'navarin', which is traditionally a splendid French spring-time stew of lamb, and applied it to pork flavoured with rosemary and juniper. It goes well with the Fennel, Mushroom and Onion Medley (see page 128).

1 kg (2 lb 4 oz) shoulder of pork, cut into 4 cm (1½ in) cubes
Salt and freshly ground black pepper
2 tbsp light olive oil
55 g (2 oz) butter
1 large onion, finely chopped
6 cloves of garlic, minced
3 tbsp plain flour
500 ml (18 fl oz) meat stock (or a chicken stock cube dissolved in 500 ml (18 fl oz) boiling water)
2 tbsp chopped flat-leaf parsley
1½ tsp juniper berries, crushed
1 tsp chopped fresh rosemary
Fresh rosemary to garnish

MARINADE
½ bottle red wine
2 cloves of garlic, lightly crushed in their skins
1 tbsp juniper berries, lightly crushed
1 tbsp fresh rosemary
A few parsley stalks

■ Put the pork cubes into a glass or china bowl and toss in the marinade ingredients. Cover and refrigerate for 6 hours or overnight.

■ Drain the pork in a colander, reserving only the liquid from the marinade in a small saucepan. Pat the meat dry with kitchen paper and season with salt and pepper.

■ Mix 1 tbsp of the oil with half the butter in a large, heavy pan and brown the meat on all sides over a high heat. Take time to do this in batches, as the browning adds both flavour and colour. When the meat is browned, sprinkle it with the flour and cook for about 5 minutes.

■ In a separate frying pan, fry the onion and garlic in the remaining oil until soft and light brown.

■ Meanwhile, gently simmer the reserved marinade. As it separates, carefully strain the clear wine liquid on to the onions, discarding the foamy residue.

■ Take the pork off the heat and add some of the meat stock, scraping the bottom of the pan for any caramelized bits and congealed flour. Add the onion mixture, remaining stock and ½ tsp salt. Bring to a very gentle simmer, cover and cook slowly for 1½–2 hours until the meat is tender.

■ To serve, add the parsley, juniper berries and chopped rosemary, then swirl in the remaining butter. Garnish with fresh rosemary.

Serves 4-6
447 cals per portion
23 g fat per portion

Stuffed loin of pork with basil

This method of opening out the meat is a good, simple technique to know, and the tasty stuffing helps the meat go a long way.

1 kg (2¼ lb) boneless loin of pork, skin and any loose bits removed

200 g (7 oz) good-quality sausages, skins removed

2 tbsp toasted pine nuts

2 tbsp chopped flat-leaf parsley

2 tbsp chopped basil

1 clove of garlic, crushed

1 tbsp vegetable oil

30 g (1¼ oz) butter

Parsley sprigs to garnish

MARINADE

2 cloves of garlic, crushed

1 tsp sugar

Salt and freshly ground black pepper

1 tbsp chopped basil

■ To prepare the pork, place it vertically in front of you, skinless side down. Using a large knife, make a downward incision to a depth of 2 cm (¾ in) along the length of the loin, 2 cm (¾ in) from the edge. Roll back the cut edge and slice horizontally through the meat, maintaining a thickness of 2 cm (¾ in). Continue cutting in this way, following the line of a circle and rolling back the meat as you go until it lies completely flat.

■ To marinate the pork, rub the inside of the meat with crushed garlic and season with sugar, salt and pepper. Sprinkle basil over the inside, cover with cling-film and chill overnight. This step is optional but gives the meat a wonderful flavour.

■ Pre-heat the oven to 220°C/425°F/Gas 7. Mix the sausage meat with the pine nuts, herbs and garlic. Remove the pork from the fridge and, using a kitchen towel, wipe off the marinade. Spread the sausage mixture over the inside of the pork, then roll it up tightly and secure with string at 2.5 cm (1 in) intervals. Season the outside of the meat.

■ Heat the vegetable oil and butter in a large oven pan until foaming, add the pork and place in the oven. For the first 10 minutes, turn the pork frequently. When it's well browned, lower the heat to 180°C/350°F/Gas 4, and cook for a further 45 minutes, turning occasionally. Remove from the oven, lightly cover with foil and allow to cool. Cut the pork into 12 even slices, garnish with parsley and serve with Ratatouille (see page 134).

Serves 6

597 cals per portion

52 g fat per portion

Navarin of pork page 105

Curried loin of pork with dried fruit

Pork fillet or tenderloin cooks quickly. It is marinated in spicy flavourings and served in a creamy sauce scattered with dried fruit.

2 pork fillets of about 800 g (1¾ lb)
    total weight
Salt and freshly ground black pepper
15 g (½ oz) butter
1 tbsp light olive oil
5 tbsp fruity white wine
330 ml (11 fl oz) coconut milk
3 tbsp double cream
Sugar and lime juice (optional), to
    season
4 dried apricots, diced
2 prunes, stoned and diced
1 tbsp currants
2 tbsp pineapple or orange juice
1 tsp concentrated tomato purée
Coconut flakes, toasted cashew nuts,
    shredded mint, to garnish

MARINADE
¼ apple, finely chopped
1 slice pineapple, skinned and
    chopped
2 tbsp soy sauce
2 tbsp curry powder
2 shallots, finely chopped
2 tbsp finely chopped ginger
Pinch cinnamon powder
6 green cardamom pods, lightly
    crushed
2 cloves
1 tbsp brown sugar

■ Trim off any fat from the pork. Combine the marinade ingredients in a large glass or china bowl, add the pork fillet and marinate for at least 2 hours and up to 8 hours.

■ Take out the pork and set the marinade aside. Pat the meat dry and season with salt and pepper.

■ Heat the butter and oil in a large sauté pan and brown the meat over a moderate heat. Cover the pan, lower the heat and cook gently, turning at least once, for 15 minutes. Transfer the cooked pork to a warm plate, cover and keep warm.

■ Pour the marinade into the pan and cook for 5 minutes over a medium high heat. Add the wine and reduce by half, then add the coconut milk and cream and bring to the boil. Take off the heat and push the pan contents through a sieve to make a smooth sauce. Season with salt and pepper plus sugar and lime juice if liked.

■ Put the apricots, prunes and currants in a bowl with the fruit juice and tomato purée, stir and cook by bringing the liquid to boiling point and simmering, covered, for 2–3 minutes.

■ To serve, slice the pork thickly and arrange it on warm plates. Spoon a little re-heated sauce around each helping and scatter over some of the fruit. Garnish with coconut flakes, toasted cashew nuts and shredded mint, and serve with couscous or rice.

Serves 4
547 cals per portion
30 g fat per portion

Grilled fillet of beef with salsa verde

In warm weather, feel free to prepare the beef on the barbecue, otherwise it's a matter of quick-sealing it on the stovetop and finishing it off in the oven. It'll taste great either way, especially with this classic Italian-style salsa verde.

750 g (1¾ lb) whole beef fillet,
   trimmed of fat and sinew
Salt and freshly ground black pepper
2 tbsp vegetable oil
Rocket leaves to garnish

SALSA VERDE
4 tbsp chopped parsley
2 tbsp good quality capers, drained
4 anchovy fillets
1 clove of garlic, chopped
1 tbsp Dijon mustard
1 tbsp lemon juice
4 tbsp virgin olive oil

■ Heat the barbecue to medium hot (i.e. when you can hold your hand over it for 3 seconds). If using the oven, pre-heat it to 200°C/400°F/Gas 6.

■ Season the beef fillet generously with salt and pepper, then rub with the oil. Brown on all sides over the hottest part of the barbecue, then move to a cooler part and cover with foil or a lid. Continue to cook, turning and checking frequently to ensure even cooking, until done to your taste – about 10 minutes for rare, about 20–25 minutes for medium to medium well done. Allow the beef to rest off the grill in a warm place for about 10 minutes before slicing.

■ To make the salsa, grind the parsley, capers, anchovies and garlic in a pestle and mortar or a food processor. When they are fairly well mixed together, add the mustard, lemon juice and virgin olive oil. Season to taste.

■ To serve, place a sliced beef fillet on each plate with a generous dollop of salsa. Garnish with the rocket leaves and serve with Grilled Potatoes and Peppers (see page 131).

Serves 4
397 cals per portion
26 g fat per portion

The Italian stallion

We first made this amazing burger when working in the wilds of Saskatchewan in Canada. A 10–20 per cent fat content is crucial for a good burger – it makes it both tender and flavoursome. Get your butcher to mince the fat for you.

750 g (1lb 10 oz) fresh lean beef, minced

150 g (5 oz) fresh kidney fat, minced

1 tsp dried oregano

1 tsp fresh thyme leaves, chopped, or ½ tsp dried thyme

2 tsp fresh parsley, chopped

1 tbsp cracked black pepper

1 tsp salt

4 slices Fontina cheese

1 large red onion, sliced thickly into rounds

1 jar of Italian roast peppers, drained

1 jar of Italian aubergine fillets, drained, or 1 fresh aubergine

4 thick slices of foccacia

4 tbsp extra virgin olive oil

Small bunch of rocket

110 g (4 oz) Italian salami, sliced

Flat-leaf parsley to garnish

ANCHOVY GARLIC MAYONNAISE

150 ml (¼ pt) store bought mayonnaise

2 cloves of garlic, minced

8 anchovy fillets, minced

2 tbsp extra virgin olive oil

■ Pre-heat the grill to high. In a large bowl, mix together the beef, fat, oregano, thyme, parsley, black pepper and salt. Work the mixture together with your hands for 1 minute.

■ Shape mixture into 4 patties and place on a baking tray under the grill. Grill for 4 minutes on each side for medium, or 6 minutes for well-done.

■ Meanwhile, mix together all the mayonnaise ingredients and season for taste. Set aside.

■ When the burgers are cooked, put in a warm place and top each with a slice of cheese. Cover with foil.

■ Place the onion, peppers and aubergine on the baking tray and grill for 2 minutes. Set aside with the burgers.

■ Toast the foccacia slices on both sides and drizzle with olive oil. Cut each slice into 2 pieces.

■ Return the burgers to the grill and heat through. Place ½ slice of foccacia on each serving plate and top with rocket, 1 tbsp of the mayonnaise and a few slices of salami. Add the burger, some vegetable slices, and more mayonnaise. Garnish and serve with remaining foccacia slice and Crispy Fried Onions (see page 136).

Serves 4

1,545 cals per portion

131 g fat per portion

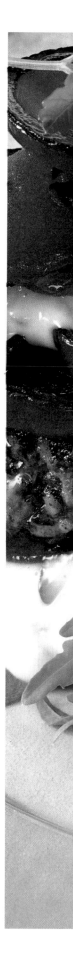

Grilled fillet of beef page 109

Roast venison page 112

Roast venison with port and cranberry sauce

Though venison is becoming more plentiful in supermarkets as well as specialist butchers and game dealers, its dark and richly flavoured meat is still a rare treat. Lean, low in cholesterol and from wild or free-range animals, a joint of venison could make a handsome alternative to turkey. Serve it with a potato gratin or, for a complete break from Christmas tradition, with Fried Polenta (see page 140).

**1.5 kg (3 lb 5 oz) boned and rolled
  haunch of venison**
2 tsp salt
2 tbsp cracked peppercorns
40 g (1½ oz) butter
2 tbsp cooking oil

SAUCE
½ bottle ruby port
Zest of 1 orange
2 tsp grated ginger
3–4 tbsp redcurrant jelly
**250 g (9 oz) fresh or frozen
  cranberries**
½ tsp salt
**150 ml (5 fl oz) homemade gravy or
  2 level tsp Bisto**
**Rosemary sprigs and sage leaves to
  garnish**

■ Pre-heat oven to 200°C/400°F/Gas 6. Cover the joint completely with sprinkled salt, and press cracked black peppercorns all over the surface. Melt the butter in the oil on top of the stove in a heavy roasting tin or a frying pan big enough to hold the joint and thoroughly brown the meat all round. This will take at least 10 minutes.

■ Transfer the joint to the oven in a roasting tin and roast for 30 minutes for medium-rare meat.

■ Meanwhile, make the sauce: bring the ruby port to the boil in a medium-sized saucepan, and add the orange zest, grated ginger and 3 tbsp of the redcurrant jelly, mashing with a spoon to help the jelly melt. Cook until reduced by half, then add the fresh or frozen cranberries, along with ¾ tsp salt. Bring the sauce back to the boil and simmer until the first cranberry bursts. Remove the pan from the heat.

■ When the venison is cooked, transfer it to a carving board and leave in a warm place to rest for at least 10 minutes. Pour off the fat from the roasting tin and stir in the gravy, or swirl 150 ml (5 fl oz) water into the tin, scraping in the meaty sediment from the bottom of the pan, then mix 2 tsp Bisto with 1 tbsp cold water and stir this in as the water in the tin comes to the boil. Stir until the mixture thickens, then add to the cranberry sauce. Simmer for 2 minutes and season, adding more redcurrant jelly if you want the sauce sweeter.

■ To serve, slice the meat, adding any juices spilled in the process to the sauce. Serve the slices on warm plates with Fried Polenta (page 140) or potatoes and greens, and pour the sauce around it. Garnish with rosemary sprigs and sage leaves.

Serves 8

390 cals per portion

12 g fat per portion

Braised shin of beef with Chinese spices

The Asian flavours lend themselves beautifully to this type of casserole and make for a really down-to-earth, warming meal.

900 g (2 lb) shin of beef, trimmed of excess fat and cut into 3 cm (1 in) cubes

6 star anise

150 ml (5 fl oz) medium sherry

6 cloves of garlic, finely sliced

4 cm (1½ in) piece of ginger, peeled and finely sliced

90 ml (3 fl oz) dark soy sauce

6 tbsp soft brown sugar

1 tsp salt

GARNISH

1 small bunch of coriander, roughly chopped

1 small bunch of spring onion, finely chopped.

■ Place the beef in 2 litres (3½ pt) water and bring to the boil. Lower the heat and simmer for 30 minutes. Skim frequently to remove any scum or froth.

■ Add the remaining ingredients and simmer partially covered for another 3 hours until the meat is very tender.

■ Uncover the pan, remove the meat with a slotted spoon, turn up the heat and cook until the sauce is reduced and slightly syrupy.

■ For the garnish, sprinkle with the coriander and spring onion. Serve with steamed jasmine or basmati rice and Chinese greens.

Serves 4

550 cals per portion

12 g fat per portion

Chargrilled and peppered chilli chicken

Hot chilli, cracked black peppercorns and sweet paprika give real bite to barbecued or grilled chicken breasts. And it's good with pork or fish, too. Serve with the Black Bean, Tomato and Avocado Salsa (see page 44).

■ Allow the chicken to come to room temperature. Light the barbecue or pre-heat the grill.

■ Meanwhile mix together the spices, herbs, seasoning and half the olive oil, then rub the mixture into the chicken. Barbecue or grill for about 8 minutes on each side, basting with the remaining oil.

Serves 4
220 cals per portion
14 g fat per portion

4 large skinned chicken breast fillets, weighing about 200 g (7 oz) each
1 tsp chilli powder
1 tsp sweet paprika
2 tsp cracked black pepper
1 tsp garlic salt
1 tbsp chopped fresh thyme (or 1 tsp dried)
1 tbsp chopped fresh parsley
½ tsp salt
4 tbsp light olive oil

Right: Chicken sauté with thai spices page 117

Breast of chicken with roast apples and ginger

It can take just minutes to dress up a plain chicken breast. By adding some ginger, chilli and a dash of soy sauce, it's instantly elevated to a really special dish. Duck or pork also works as a good substitute for the chicken.

6 chicken breast fillets, weighing about 170 g (6 oz) each
Salt and freshly ground black pepper
1 tbsp light olive oil
2 tbsp butter
350 ml (12 fl oz) cider
Apple peels and core (reserved from roasting apples)
1.5 cm (½ in) piece of fresh ginger, finely chopped
1 tbsp soy sauce
Pinch chilli flakes
1 tbsp demerara sugar
150 ml (5 fl oz) chicken stock
Fresh herbs to garnish

ROAST APPLES
3 Cox Pippin or Granny Smith apples, peeled and cored (reserve peels and core)
Splash of dry cider
2 tbsp butter
2 tbsp demerara sugar

★ The apples can be prepared in advance and then re-heated.

■ Season the chicken fillets generously with salt and pepper. Heat a large frying pan over a fairly high heat, add the olive oil and half the butter and fry until the butter has browned slightly. Add the chicken fillets skin-side down, and cook for a further 8 minutes on each side, making sure they don't brown too much.

■ Meanwhile, place the cider and the reserved apple peels and cores in a saucepan and boil until reduced by two thirds. Strain the reduced liquid through a fine sieve into a clean saucepan, pressing down on the apple trimmings to extract all the juices. Add the ginger, soy sauce, chilli, sugar and chicken stock, bring to the boil and simmer for 5 minutes until reduced a little. Stir in the remaining butter and season to taste. Strain and keep warm.

■ To roast the apples, cut into eighths and sprinkle with a good splash of cider. Heat a heavy frying pan over a high heat and add the butter and sugar, allowing the butter to sizzle. Add the apples and cook for 10 minutes, turning them frequently, until the apples are brown and tender when pierced with the point of a knife.

■ To serve, place each chicken fillet on a warm plate with segments of the roasted apple. Pour the sauce over the chicken and garnish with a few fresh herbs. Serve with a pilau rice and a small salad.

Serves 6
362 cals per protion
10 g fat per portion

Chicken sauté with thai spices

A richly spiced and gloriously creamy chicken dish that's delicious served with peppery Chinese greens and a Crispy Noodle Pancake (see page 141).

1.4 kg (3 lb) chicken, cut into 10
 serving pieces
Salt and freshly ground black pepper
15 g (½ oz) butter
2 tbsp vegetable oil
270 ml (9 fl oz) chicken stock
6 lime leaves
5 cm (2 in) piece fresh galangal spice
 (or 1 tbsp dried pieces)
210 ml (7 fl oz) coconut milk
2 serrano chillies, sliced
2 tbsp Thai fish sauce
½ tsp cracked black peppercorns
150 ml (5 fl oz) whipping cream
1 red pepper, de-seeded and cut into
 strips
6–8 shitake mushrooms, sliced
2 tbsp fresh coriander, chopped
1–2 tbsp lime juice
Steamed bok choy or other Chinese
 cabbage greens to serve

■ Season the chicken with salt and pepper. Melt the butter in half the oil in a large casserole dish and brown the chicken over a moderately high heat. Cover the pan, turn the heat to low, and cook, turning the chicken occasionally, for 25–30 minutes.

■ Meanwhile, bring the chicken stock to the boil with the lime leaves and galangal. Turn off the heat and leave to infuse. When the chicken is cooked, transfer the pieces to a warm dish, pour off the fat from the casserole and strain in the infused chicken stock.

■ Boil vigorously to reduce the stock by about a half. Add the coconut milk, chillies, fish sauce, black peppercorns and cream. Boil until the sauce thickens slightly. Meanwhile, stir-fry the pepper strips and shitake mushrooms lightly in the remaining vegetable oil.

■ Reheat the chicken pieces in the casserole. Finally add the coriander and lime juice. Serve, garnished with pepper strips, shitake mushrooms and steamed greens, accompanied by a slice of Crispy Noodle Pancake.

Serves 4

785 cals per portion
64 g fat per portion

Chicken with lime and chilli lentils

This is really two recipes. The lentils work very well with grilled fish; the marinated chicken could also be served with a rice dish. Both taste great served warm or at room temperature, so are perfect for taking on a picnic.

MARINADE
1 lemon grass stalk, crushed and
   roughly chopped
1 clove of garlic, chopped
2.5 cm (1 in) piece of fresh ginger,
   chopped
2 tbsp light soy sauce
1 tbsp sugar
Pinch of chilli powder (optional)
Salt and freshly ground black pepper

CHICKEN
4 boned, skinned chicken breasts,
   each weighing about 150 to 175 g
   (5–6 oz)
2 tbsp vegetable oil

LENTILS
100 g (3½ oz) Puy lentils
0.75 litre (1½–1¾ pt) water or
   stock
1 tsp salt
½ onion, finely chopped
½ carrot, finely chopped
½ celery stalk, finely chopped

DRESSING
Juice and zest of 1 lime
1–2 chillies, finely diced
1 clove of garlic, minced
100 ml (3½ fl oz) extra virgin olive
   oil
4 tbsp fresh coriander, chopped
Fresh coriander sprigs to garnish

■ Mix together all the marinade ingredients in a shallow bowl. Add the chicken breasts to the marinade and leave in the fridge, preferably overnight, turning once or twice.

■ Remove the chicken from the marinade. Heat a heavy frying pan over a high heat and add the oil. Start by cooking the chicken breasts over a high heat then reduce to a medium heat. Cook for about 6 minutes on each side. Test the chicken with a skewer to see if it's cooked.

■ Rinse the lentils in cold water, then put them into a medium saucepan with the water or stock and 1 tsp salt. Bring to the boil, add the vegetables, cover and simmer gently for 10–15 minutes. Remove the pan from the heat and leave to cool slightly.

■ Meanwhile, make the dressing by simply mixing together all the ingredients, except the coriander. Drain the lentils and place in a bowl. Pour over the dressing, season and leave to infuse. Toss in the chopped coriander.

■ To serve, place 1–2 spoonfuls of the lentils on warmed plates. Place a chicken breast in the centre of the lentils and garnish with fresh coriander and Roasted Aubergines (see page 134).

Serves 4
559 cals per portion
36 g fat per portion

Glazed duck breast with lime, pickled ginger and soy sauce

Duck is highly prized in Pacific Rim cooking because the fatty layer contributes flavour and succulence, and insulates the meat during cooking. This dish has an authentic Eastern slant without any chilli heat.

4 Barbary duck breasts, about 175 g (6 oz) each
Salt and freshly ground white pepper
2 medium-sized limes
2 tbsp golden syrup
2 tbsp soy sauce
2 tbsp granulated sugar
2 tbsp pickled ginger, cut into strips
Sliced spring onion to garnish
Steamed bok choy and rice to serve

★ Japanese soy sauce is naturally fermented and is usually better quality.

★ You can find pickled ginger in Oriental supermarkets, and the Japanese or Chinese variety works well here. You can substitute with a piece of ginger preserved in syrup – reduce the syrup content of the sauce slightly.

■ With a sharp knife, lightly score the skin of each duck breast in a criss-cross pattern. Season and leave to reach room temperature.

■ Thinly pare the zest from the limes and shred into strips. Squeeze about 2 tbsp of juice from the limes. Mix the golden syrup, soy sauce and lime juice together, and leave to one side. Bring the strips of lime to the boil in 300 ml (½ pt) water. Simmer for 10 minutes, then drain and add a fresh 100 ml (3½ fl oz) water and the granulated sugar. Bring to the boil and simmer for a further 15 minutes. Make sure the water doesn't evaporate completely and add a splash more if needed. Add the ginger and leave to one side.

■ Heat a large frying pan over a moderate heat and cook the duck breasts skin-side down for about 5 minutes until the skin is golden. Turn and cook a further 2–3 minutes for medium-rare meat. Pour off the fat and turn skin-side down again. Add both the soy mixture and the lime and ginger mixture. Allow the liquid to bubble up until the duck is glazed.

■ Carve each piece of duck into 4 or 5 neat slices on a board. Arrange in the centre of warm serving plates and add a little sauce to each.

■ Garnish with sliced spring onion and serve with steamed bok choy and rice.

Serves 4
408 cals per portion
20 g fat per portion

Chargrilled breast of duck with green peppercorns and mango salsa

This is a great barbecue dish – tasty and easy to master – but you can cook it under the grill if the weather lets you down. It's best to make the salsa ahead of time to allow the flavours to develop. If you can't find green peppercorns, use black ones instead.

4 small Barbary duck breasts
Salt to taste
Freshly ground green peppercorns

MANGO SALSA
4 tbsp red onion, finely chopped
2 ripe mangoes, peeled and cut into
   1 cm (½ in) dice
4 tbsp lime or lemon juice
1–2 red chillies, finely diced
1 tbsp sugar
2 tbsp fresh mint, chopped
½ tsp salt
Freshly ground green peppercorns
Flat-leaf parsley to garnish

■ Light the barbecue and leave to heat up. Season the duck breasts with salt and freshly ground green peppercorns, then place them, skin-side down, on a fairly cool spot on the barbecue. When the skin begins to crisp, it will exude fat which will cause the barbecue to flare up. If this happens, spray with a little water to kill off the flames. At this point, turn the duck breasts and move them away from the flame. Cook for a few minutes, skin-side up, then turn them again to crisp up the skin. Continue this process until the duck is cooked to your taste.

■ To make the salsa, first scald the red onion by pouring boiling water over it and draining it off immediately. (This softens the raw flavour of the onion, which can slightly overpower the other ingredients.) Mix together with the remaining salsa ingredients and allow the flavours to combine for ½ hour. Taste the salsa, adding a little more lime, sugar or salt if desired.

■ Garnish the duck breasts with parsley and serve with plenty of salsa on the side. This dish goes very well with Wild Rice Pilau (see page 137).

Serves 4
413 cals per portion
23 g fat per portion

Guinea fowl with wild mushrooms

Guinea fowl is a delicious, slightly firmer version of chicken.

1 small fresh thyme sprig
4 cloves of garlic, unpeeled and
    lightly crushed
1 large guinea fowl, weighing about
    1.5 kg (3 lb 5 oz)
Salt and freshly ground black pepper
4 tbsp light olive oil
Buttered cabbage to garnish

SAUCE
100 ml (3 fl oz) Madeira or port
250 ml (9 fl oz) brown chicken or
    beef stock
250 g (9 oz) wild mushrooms, such
    as chanterelles, oysters, shitake
Pinch of salt
2 tbsp butter
½ tsp fresh thyme leaves
½ tbsp chopped fresh parsley

■ Pre-heat the oven to 200°C/400°F/Gas 6. Place the thyme and garlic inside the guinea fowl and season inside and out. Heat 2 tbsp of the oil in a roasting tin in the oven. Place the guinea fowl on its side in the tin and roast for 10 minutes.

■ Turn the guinea fowl on to its other side and continue to roast for 10 minutes. Turn the guinea fowl breast-side up, lower the oven temperature to 180°C/350°F/Gas 4, and roast for 20 minutes.

■ Remove the guinea fowl from the oven, transfer to a clean dish, cover with foil and allow to rest for 15 minutes. Pour the fat from the roasting pan and deglaze the pan with Madeira or port. Tip the juices into a saucepan and add the stock. Boil until reduced by half.

■ Heat a large frying pan over a high heat, add the remaining oil and fry the mushrooms with a little salt for 3–4 minutes. Tip on to a roasting tray. Cut the legs off the guinea fowl and place on the roasting tray with the mushrooms. Cut down the side of the breastbone and remove the breasts. Place on the roasting tray.

■ To serve, warm the mushrooms and guinea fowl in the oven for 3–4 minutes. Meanwhile, bring the sauce to the boil, then whisk in the butter and herbs. Season to taste.

■ Place a little cabbage and some mushrooms on each warmed plate. Top with the guinea fowl and pour over the sauce. Serve with Roast Garlic Bubble and Squeak (see page 135).

Serves 4
712 cals per portion
39 g fat per portion

Braised duck legs with red wine

Served with seasonal vegetables, this makes a hearty main course. Add mashed potatoes if you wish.

**4 Barbary duck legs, each weighing
about 200 g (7 oz)**
Salt and freshly ground black pepper
1 tbsp light olive oil
2 shallots, roughly chopped
1 carrot, roughly chopped
2 cloves of garlic, lightly crushed
1 bouquet garni
½ bottle red wine
500 ml (18 fl oz) chicken stock
2 tsp sugar

■ Pre-heat the oven to 180°C/350°F/Gas 4. Season the duck legs, then heat the oil in a large, heavy casserole. Brown the duck legs well on both sides over a medium heat, then remove and keep warm. Pour off all but 1 tbsp of the fat.

■ Add the shallots, carrot and garlic to the casserole and sauté until lightly browned. Add the bouquet garni and red wine, and boil until the wine has reduced to a syrup. Add the stock, 1tsp sugar, the duck legs and a good pinch of salt. Bring to a simmer, cover and cook in the oven for 1¼ hours, or until tender.

■ Place the duck legs on a warm plate. Pass sauce through a sieve, then simmer over a high heat until it has a light syrupy consistency. Season to taste with salt, pepper and the remaining sugar. Replace the duck legs and heat through.

■ Serve on a bed of seasonal greens, cooked briefly and tossed in butter, surrounded with the sauce. This dish goes well with Glazed Turnips with Bacon and Onion (see page 136).

Serves 4
519 cals per portion
39 g fat per portion

Pigeon breast with sage and black pepper

Pigeons are the bargain of the game counter, available all year round. Their breasts are tender and delicate and need the briefest of cooking, while the legs contribute deep, gamey flavour to the sauce.

4 pigeons
2 tbsp light olive oil
½ medium onion, finely chopped
1 small carrot, finely chopped
½ stick of celery, finely chopped
1 clove of garlic, crushed
1 bay leaf
4 juniper berries
8 black peppercorns
120 ml (4 fl oz) red wine
240 ml (8 fl oz) chicken stock
½ tsp cracked black peppercorns
1 tsp chopped fresh sage
25 g (1 oz) butter
Buttered spinach or cabbage to
  accompany
4 sprigs fresh sage, to garnish

■ With a sharp, pointed knife, cut breasts from the pigeon, keeping your knife towards the bones all the time. Trim the fillets into a nice shape and set aside.

■ Chop the carcasses with a heavy knife and brown well in 1 tbsp olive oil. Add the vegetables, garlic, bay leaf, juniper berries and whole peppercorns and cook for another 5 minutes. Stir in the wine, scraping the base of the pan to release the tasty bits, and cook to reduce the wine until it has almost disappeared.

■ Add the stock, bring to the boil and simmer for 15 minutes. Strain through a fine sieve into a clean pan, stir in the cracked peppercorns, fresh sage and half the butter, taste and add more salt if necessary.

■ To cook the pigeon breasts, heat the remaining butter and oil together in a large frying pan. Season the breasts with salt and pepper and when the butter is foaming, add them skin-side down and adjust the heat – they should brown slowly without hardening to crispness. Cook for about 4 minutes on one side, turn and cook for 2 minutes on the other side for medium-rare meat.

■ Place on a warm plate to rest for 2 minutes, then remove the skin and slice each breast in half. Arrange on top of buttered spinach or cabbage, spoon a little sauce over and decorate each with a sage sprig.

Serves 4
385 cals per portion
26 g fat per portion

Fennel, mushroom and onion medley page 128

vegetables

Glazed turnips with bacon and onion page 136

Crispy noodle pancake page 141

Crispy fried onions page 136

Sautéed potato with prunes and apples page 132

& side dishes

Fennel, mushroom and onion medley

A delicious winter vegetable mix to serve with main-course stews or on its own as a dressing for pasta.

280 g (10 oz) baby onions
1 large fennel bulb
25 g (1 oz) butter
1 tbsp olive oil
½ tsp sugar
125 g (4 oz) button mushrooms, stems trimmed
Salt and freshly ground black pepper

■ Peel the baby onions, leaving on the tops of the roots to keep them from falling apart. (Peeling is easier if you soak the onions in very hot water for 10 minutes first.) If the onions are quite large, cut them in half before you peel them – this makes the peeling easier, too.

■ Trim the top off the fennel bulb and quarter it lengthways. Cut out and discard the core and halve the 'leaves' of fennel in half again lengthways.

■ Heat the butter with the oil in a large saucepan over a medium heat until it turns golden brown. Add the fennel, baby onions and sugar and sauté for 4–5 minutes until nicely browned. Add the button mushrooms and season. Cover and cook for 5 minutes, stirring occasionally, and adjusting the heat as necessary. Serve immediately.

Serves 4-6
107 cals per portion
8 g fat per portion

Gratin of pumpkin

A soft, sweet golden dish that's great with all our winter game dishes, and with lamb.

750 g (1½ lb) pumpkin
25 g (1 oz) butter
Salt and freshly ground black pepper
1 large clove of garlic, halved
300 ml (10 fl oz) double cream
Pinch of grated nutmeg
1 tbsp chopped parsley
1½ tsp chopped fresh sage
2 tbsp grated Parmesan

■ Preheat the oven to 200°C/400°F/Gas 6. Peel the pumpkin and remove the seeds and central fibre. Cut into 2 cm (about 1 in) cubes and sauté in a large frying pan with the butter, salt and pepper. Cook for about 5 minutes until golden.

■ Sprinkle a small casserole or gratin dish with a little salt and rub it all over with the cut side of the garlic. Tip in the pumpkin. Bring the cream to the boil, add a little salt, the nutmeg, parsley and sage. Pour over the pumpkin, sprinkle with Parmesan and bake for 10–15 minutes until golden on top.

Serves 4–6
429 cals per prtion
43 g fat per portion

New potatoes with garlic and peas

If you don't have fresh garden peas and broad beans use frozen vegetables in buttery combinations instead.

700 g (1½ lb) new potatoes
36 cloves of garlic, unpeeled
80g (3 oz) butter
3 tbsp light olive oil
Salt
200 g (7 oz) fresh or frozen shelled peas
200 g (7 oz) fresh or frozen shelled broad beans

■ Scrub or scrape the potatoes, whichever you prefer, but make sure you dry them well before cooking. Separate the cloves of garlic without peeling them and simmer in water in a small saucepan for about 3 minutes, then drain well.

■ In a large pan or casserole, heat the butter and oil until the butter foams. Add the potatoes and cook until they are light brown. Add the garlic and some salt, cover, reduce the heat slightly and cook for 15 minutes, shaking the pan occasionally.

■ Cook the peas and beans separately in water until just tender – frozen scarcely need more than to be brought to the boil (or cook them in the microwave). Drain and stir into the potatoes and garlic.

■ To serve, drain off excess butter and spoon the vegetables on to warm plates.

Serves 6
296 cals per portion
18 g fat per portion

Grilled potatoes and peppers

Vegetables always taste fabulous cooked on the barbecue – the chargrilling adds so much flavour. Alternatively, you could cook them under a hot grill.

4 medium-sized potatoes with skin left on, baked or boiled

Olive oil for brushing

1 red pepper, quartered and seeded

1 yellow pepper, quartered and seeded

Salt and freshly ground black pepper

3 tbsp chopped fresh herbs, such as thyme and parsley

■ Heat the barbecue past its hottest stage, but still a good medium hot heat. Halve the potatoes lengthways and brush generously with olive oil.

■ Brush the quartered peppers with olive oil and season to taste. Place on the barbecue and leave for about 2–3 minutes until well marked by the grill. Place the potatoes on the grill and roast for 5 minutes until well heated through. If you prefer, the skin of the peppers, now blackened and shrivelled, can be removed before serving.

■ To serve, arrange the vegetables on a serving plate, drizzle with a little more olive oil and sprinkle with the freshly chopped herbs.

Serves 4
239 cals per portion
6 g fat per portion

Sautéed potatoes with prunes and apples

This interesting potato dish suits most meats, especially lamb (see page 104). It's also great as a quick brunch with crispy grilled streaky bacon.

8 small stoneless prunes

75 ml (2½ fl oz) chicken stock

500 g (1 lb 2 oz) medium potatoes, unpeeled

3 tbsp butter

1 large apple, peeled, cored and diced into 2.5 cm (1 in) chunks

Pinch of sugar

1 small red onion, sliced thinly lengthways

Salt and freshly ground black pepper

1 tbsp slivered almonds, toasted

■ Place the prunes in a small saucepan with the chicken stock. Bring to the boil and simmer for 1 minute. Set aside. Cook the potatoes in their skins in salted water, then drain and allow to cool. Peel the potatoes and cut into 2.5 cm (1 in) chunks.

■ Melt the butter in a large frying pan, add the apple and sugar and sauté until the apple is lightly browned. Add the potatoes, onion, and a little salt and pepper, and continue to cook until the potatoes are lightly browned.

■ Add the prunes and heat through – don't worry if they break up a little. Sprinkle with the toasted almonds and serve with the Morroccan Lamb Kebabs.

Serves 4

239 cals per portion

11 g fat per portion

Vegetable medley

This is not so much a recipe, as a simple cooking technique.

125 g (4 oz) carrots, sliced

125 g (4 oz) green beans, trimmed

125 g (4 oz) asparagus tips

125 g (4 oz) cauliflower, broken into
  small florets

125 g (4 oz) broccoli, broken into
  small florets

Salt and freshly ground black pepper

2–4 tbsp butter

■ The carrots will take about 5 minutes to cook; the green beans about 4 minutes; the asparagus tips, 3 minutes; the cauliflower about 2 minutes; and the broccoli florets only 1 minute.

■ Bring a large pan of salted water to the boil. Start by adding the carrots to the pan then, after each minute, add the next vegetable. Repeat this with each type of vegetable until they are all cooked. Drain them well then toss in butter.

■ The vegetables can be cooked, rinsed with cold water, drained and tossed in butter ahead of time. When ready to serve, simply re-heat the vegetables in the microwave and season well with salt and ground black pepper.

Serves 4

92 cals per portion

7 g fat per portion

Ratatouille

Superb for vegetarians or meat eaters, this ratatouille is bursting with flavours. Serve it with the Stuffed Loin of Pork (see page 106), pulses or fish.

1 medium onion, finely chopped
120 ml (4 fl oz) light olive oil
Salt and freshly ground black pepper
½ red pepper, de-seeded and finely diced
½ yellow pepper, deseeded and finely diced
6 plum tomatoes, peeled, deseeded and roughly diced
2 cloves of garlic, finely chopped
Fresh thyme sprig, chopped, or about ½ tsp dried thyme
2 medium courgettes, cut into 1 cm (½ in) dice
1 aubergine, cut into 1 cm (½ in) dice

■ Sweat the onion in a saucepan with 2 tbsp olive oil and a pinch of salt until soft and translucent. Add the peppers and cook for 5 minutes, then add the tomatoes, garlic and thyme. Cover and continue cooking.

■ Meanwhile, warm 2 tbsp olive oil in a large frying pan over a high heat. Add the courgettes, cook until lightly browned, then tip into a colander to drain off the excess oil.

■ Heat the remaining olive oil in the same pan. Add the aubergine, brown and drain. Sprinkle the aubergine and courgettes with a little salt, then add them to the onion, pepper and tomato mixture. Cover and cook for 10 minutes. Serve hot or cold, by itself, or with an accompanying dish.

Serves 6
197 cals per portion
18 g fat per portion

Roasted aubergine

Pork fillet or tenderloin cooks quickly. It is marinated in spicy flavourings and served in a creamy sauce scattered with dried fruit.

1 aubergine, weighing about 200 g (7 oz)
Salt and freshly ground black pepper
2 tbsp vegetable oil

GLAZE
2 tbsp Japanese soy sauce
1 tbsp sugar
1 tbsp water

■ Pre-heat the oven to 180°C/350°F/Gas 4. Cut off the ends of the aubergine, then cut crossways into 4 equal slices. Using a pointed knife, score both sides of the flesh. Lightly season each slice with salt and pepper then brush with vegetable oil and place on a metal baking sheet.

■ Mix together all the glaze ingredients and spoon a little over the top of the aubergine slices.

Cook in the oven for about 15 minutes, turning occasionally and basting with a little glaze every 2–3 minutes, until slices are very tender. This will take about 25–30 minutes in total.

Serves 4
76 cals per portion
6 g fat per portion

Roast garlic bubble and squeak

This old favourite is even better with the addition of subtle, creamy roast garlic. We store the purée in the fridge covered with olive oil.

6–8 cloves of garlic, unpeeled
2 tbsp light olive oil
3 tbsp butter
2 tbsp chopped onion
1 large handful of cooked, chopped cabbage
750 g (1 lb 10 oz) cooked potatoes
Salt and ground black pepper
Flour for dusting

■ Pre-heat the oven to 180°C/350°F/Gas 4. Place the garlic cloves on a piece of foil and drizzle with 1 tbsp of the light olive oil. Scrunch up the foil into a purse and cook in the oven for 45 minutes. Remove and allow to cool.

■ Open the foil and carefully squeeze the garlic cloves from the skins.

■ Melt 2 tbsp of the butter in a large pan and sauté the onion and cabbage for about 3 minutes. Tip into a large bowl with the garlic cloves. Allow to cool slightly, then add the potatoes. Mix together using your hands, crushing the potatoes roughly. Season well. Shape the mixture into 4–6 balls, dust with flour and press into neat patties.

■ Heat the remaining oil and butter in a frying pan until foaming. Add the patties and cook over a moderate heat for 3 minutes on each side. Serve immediately.

Serves 4–6
286 cals per portion
15 g fat per portion

Crispy fried onions

One of our all-time favourites, this is good with almost everything!

4 large Spanish onions
1 tsp salt
Flour for dredging
Oil for deep-frying

■ Cut the onions in half lengthways from root to point. Place in a bowl, and sprinkle with salt. Separate the pieces with your hands, leave for 2–3 minutes, then toss in the flour, pressing it into the slices to form a crust.

■ Deep-fry the onion slices in hot oil at 180°C/350°F until golden.

Serves 4
321 cals per portion
25 g fat per portion

Glazed turnips with bacon and onion

This is a great accompaniment to any meat dish. It's best to use smaller turnips for their wonderful flavour.

1 tbsp butter
6 rashers smoked streaky bacon
255 g (9 oz) peeled young white turnips, trimmed if small and quartered if large
1 tsp sugar
Salt and freshly ground black pepper
1 small onion, sliced into thin rounds
1 tbsp freshly chopped parsley

■ Melt the butter in a medium saucepan. Slice the bacon into thin strips and fry in the butter until golden. Remove and keep warm.

■ Add the turnips to the remaining fat in the pan with 2 tbsp water, the sugar and a little salt. Cover and cook until the turnips are just tender, then remove the lid and add the onion. Cook over medium heat until the onions are cooked through and the turnips have a little colour.

■ Place bacon back in pan and heat through. Serve sprinkled with the parsley and pepper.

Serves 4
180 cals per portion
15 g fat per portion

Wild rice pilau

Wild rice is an expensive luxury, but it's easy to cook and is absolutely delicious. However, we feel it needs enhancing with other vegetables or flavourings, so here we've used spring onions and mushrooms to lighten the texture and add taste.

250 g (9 oz) wild rice
700 ml (1¼ pt) stock, made from
  vegetable or chicken stock cubes
4 tbsp butter
200 g (7 oz) button mushrooms,
  finely sliced
6 medium spring onions, finely sliced

■ Rinse the rice in plenty of cold water. Place in a saucepan with the stock and bring to the boil. Taste and add salt if necessary (but remember that stock cubes are salty). Cover and cook gently for 40–45 minutes. The rice is cooked when the grains have split slightly, but if they are still too hard, give them a little longer before draining off any remaining liquid.

■ While the rice is cooking, melt the butter in a large saucepan. Add the mushrooms and spring onions. Cook over a high heat for 3–4 minutes.

■ Add the cooked rice to the pan and fold in the vegetables. Serve immediately, or allow to cool and reheat in the microwave when needed.

Serves 4
349 cals per portion
14 g fat per portion

Coconut rice

Delicately flavoured with coconut, these cones of rice are easy to do and will make any dish look spectacular.

300 g (10¾ oz) long grain or
** jasmine rice**
400 g (14 oz) can of coconut milk
Pinch of salt
1 spring onion, finely shredded and
** soaked in cold water**

■ Wash the rice well, drain, place in a heavy-based saucepan with the coconut milk, 200 ml (7 fl oz) water and a good pinch of salt. Bring to the boil, stir once and cover. Turn the heat down very low (if necessary, use a heat-resistant mat) and cook gently for 15 minutes. Remove from the heat, leave to stand for 10 minutes, then fluff up with a fork.

■ While the rice is cooking, make the moulds for the cones. Take 4 sheets of silicone paper, 24.5 cm sq (9½ in sq), fold each into a triangle, bring the edges together to form a cone and secure by rolling down the top edge to make a cone 11 cm (4½ in) high. When the rice is cooked, spoon a little at a time into each cone, pushing it down well and levelling off when full. Carefully turn each cone of rice on to a serving place. Dicard the paper and garnish with the spring onion.

Serves 4
293 cals per portion
1 g fat per portion

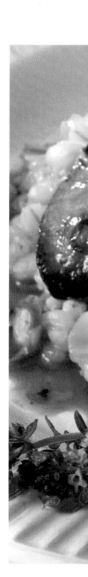

Saffron and barley risotto

The creaminess of the barley copies authentic risotto with great success. We added saffron, but feel free to use other vegetables, spices or herbs.

150 g (5 oz) barley
50 g (2 oz) butter
1 small onion, finely chopped
40 g (1½ oz) carrots, finely sliced
40 g (1½ oz) celery, finely sliced
Salt and freshly ground black pepper
Pinch of saffron threads
1 litre (1¾ pt) hot chicken stock
50 ml (1½ fl oz) double cream

■ Rinse the barley well and allow to drain. Melt 15 g (½ oz) of the butter in a pan, add the vegetables and a little salt. Sweat for 3–4 minutes until soft. Add the saffron and barley and continue to cook for 1 minute.

■ Pour in enough chicken stock to cover the barley and simmer gently. Cook, uncovered, for 20–25 minutes, stirring every 2–3 minutes until the barley is cooked. As the liquid evaporates, add more stock. If you want to make the risotto ahead, this is where you stop cooking. To reheat, cook gently in the microwave or over a very low heat, adding a little more stock. Stir frequently.

■ To finish, add the double cream and stir in the remaining butter. Season to taste and serve.

Serves 4
302 cals per portion
17 g fat per portion

Fried polenta with onion and sage

We entirely disagree with those who find polenta bland: it's the perfect accompaniment for rich stews and roasts, and you can add flavourings to suit the meat. We love it and are constantly coming up with new versions like this sage and onion one, which is great with pork, duck or our venison roast. Its hidden advantage for busy Christmas cooks is that the polenta has to be made in advance.

55 g (2 oz) butter

1 tbsp light olive oil

2 large onions, finely sliced

1½ tsp dried sage (or 1 tbsp fresh chopped sage)

Salt and freshly ground black pepper

250 g (9 oz) instant polenta

4 tbsp grated Parmesan

■ Melt half the butter with the light olive oil in a large frying pan over a medium heat. Add the onion slices, dried sage (if that's what you're using) and a little salt. Fry gently for about 10 minutes, stirring regularly, until the onions are soft and golden brown. If you are using fresh sage, add it to the pan now and set aside.

■ Bring 1 litre (1¾ pt) cold water to the boil in a large saucepan and add a little salt. Trickle the instant polenta into the water in a steady stream, stirring constantly. Cook for about 7 minutes, stirring frequently. The polenta is cooked when it loses its graininess and begins to come away from the sides of the pan. Stir in the grated Parmesan, along with the onion and sage mixture. Season to taste.

■ Lightly grease a ceramic dish and spoon in the cooked polenta, pressing it down in a flat layer. Cover with a sheet of greaseproof and leave to set, then transfer to the fridge where it will keep for 3–4 days.

■ Turn the chilled polenta out of the dish on to a board and cut into thick slices or, if you prefer, use a scone cutter to make neat discs. Melt the remaining butter in a heavy frying pan (preferably a non-stick one) and, when it sizzles, add the polenta slices and fry until crisp and brown on both sides. Serve hot.

Serves 8

211 cals per portion

9 g fat per portion

Crispy noodle pancake

You can make the pancake in advance and reheat in an oven pre-heated to 180°C/350°F/Gas 4.

225 g (8 oz) thin Chinese egg
   noodles
1 tsp toasted sesame seed oil
2 tbsp soy sauce
2 tbsp vegetable oil

■ Cook the noodles according to the packet instructions, refresh in cold water, drain in a colander and pat dry on paper towel. Transfer to a bowl, season with sesame oil and soy sauce, and toss well.

■ Heat the vegetable oil in a medium-sized sauté pan and shape the noodles into a cake in the pan, pressing them down to a thickness of about 1.5 cm (½ in).

■ Fry for 4–5 minutes on either side, adding more oil for the flip side, until golden brown. Sizzle without scorching. Slip the cooked cake on to 2 layers of paper towel to drain.

Serves 4
303 cals per portion
13 g fat per portion

Warm apple and hazelnut streusel galette page 145

Soft fruit and mascarpone trifle page 152

puddings

Pear and apple corn meal crumble

Use both or either fruits for this crumble. The nuttiness of the corn meal adds depth to the topping, and although we use almonds, feel free to substitute hazelnuts instead.

Juice and zest of 1 lemon

3 Golden Delicious or Granny Smith apples

4 ripe Comice or Conference pears

3 tbsp unsalted butter

6 tbsp sugar

1 tbsp plain flour

40 g (1½ oz) toasted ground almonds

CRUMBLE TOPPING

55 g (2 oz) white sugar

55 g (2 oz) golden demerara sugar

50 g (1¾ oz) plain flour

50 g (1¾ oz) fine corn meal

100 g (3½ oz) unsalted butter, diced

60 g (2 oz) chopped almonds

■ Pre-heat the oven to 190°C/375°F/Gas 5. Place the lemon juice in a small bowl, reserving the zest, then peel the fruit, rolling it in the lemon juice to avoid discolouration. Roughly dice the apples and pears, then place in separate bowls with the lemon juice.

■ Heat a large frying pan over a medium heat and add 1½ tbsp of the butter. When it has stopped foaming, add the apples and cook for about 3 minutes, shaking the pan to prevent them sticking. Add half the sugar and cook for a further 3–5 minutes. When ready, the apples should be quite soft and almost golden. Take off the heat, drain off excess liquid and reserve. Repeat with the pears.

■ Mix the cooked fruits together with the flour and lemon zest, then set aside to cool slightly.

■ To make the crumble topping, mix together all the ingredients, except the chopped almonds, with your fingertips or in a food processor, until the mixture forms large crumbs.

■ Sprinkle the toasted ground almonds in a shallow ovenproof dish about 22.5 cm by 15 cm (9 in by 6 in) and lay the cooked fruits on top. Sprinkle the crumble topping over the fruit and scatter with the chopped almonds. Cook in the oven for 25–30 minutes, until firm and golden. Meanwhile, boil the reserved fruit liquid until reduced to a syrupy consistency.

■ Serve the crumble on warmed plates with single cream spooned around and dotted with the reduced fruit syrup; or with crème fraîche or ice-cream, if preferred.

Serves 4–6

802 cals per portion

44 g fat per portion

Warm apple and hazelnut streusel galette with fresh blackberry sauce

With crisp puff pastry and a hazelnut topping, apples have never tasted better.

175 g (6 oz) ready-made puff pastry
4 large Granny Smith apples, peeled
** and grated**
4 tbsp sugar
4 tsp lemon juice
1 tbsp melted butter
Mint sprigs to decorate

STREUSEL
75 g (3 oz) plain flour
75 g (3 oz) golden brown sugar
75 g (3 oz) hazelnut kernels, toasted
75 g (3 oz) cold butter, diced
2 tsp grated zest of lemon or lime

SAUCE
175 g (6 oz) fresh blackberries
2–4 tbsp sugar

■ Roll out the pastry 0.5 cm (¼ in) thick, making a sheet about 40 x 25 cm (16 x 10 in) and refrigerate for at least 20 minutes while the oven pre-heats to 190°C/375°F/Gas 5.

■ Toss the apples with the sugar and lemon juice, and leave to stand in a bowl for about 15 minutes. Put all the streusel ingredients into a food processor and pulse until the mixture is the consistency of coarse breadcrumbs, then set aside.

■ Trim the edges of the chilled pastry to make a neat rectangle, then lay it on a baking sheet and prick all over the surface with a fork to stop it puffing up too much. Bake in the oven until the pastry starts to turn golden brown. This will take about 10 minutes. Remove from the oven, cool slightly then brush with the melted butter.

■ Strain off the excess liquid from the apples by pressing them gently in a sieve – you should have about 110 ml (4 fl oz) juice. Put this to one side. Spread the grated apple over the pastry to within about 0.5 cm (¼ in) of the edges. Sprinkle the streusel generously over the apples, return to the oven and bake until the top is golden brown and crisp – about a further 20 minutes.

■ Meanwhile, make the sauce. Reserving a few blackberries for decoration, blend the rest with the reserved juice from the apples and sweeten to taste. Sieve and taste again, adding a little lemon juice or more sugar.

■ Cut the galette into individual portions and decorate with the remaining blackberries and mint. Serve with blackberry sauce or a dollop of cream.

Serves 6
493 cals per portion
26.78 g fat per portion

Pear and apple corn meal crumble page 144

Deep dish sour cream and apple pie page 148

Deep dish sour cream and apple pie

Growing up on the Canadian prairies, this was our traditional dessert at Christmas time. We flavoured it with cinnamon, although you could use nutmeg or allspice. Some people like it served with Cheddar cheese, but a dollop of whipped cream or ice cream also works well. Use a 23 cm (9 in) wide and 2½ cm (1 in) deep fluted flan tin or buy a pre-baked pastry shell.

PASTRY

110 g (4 oz) chilled unsalted butter, diced

175 g (6 oz) plain flour

Pinch of salt

55 g (2 oz) caster sugar

1 egg yolk

½ tbsp double cream

FILLING

900 g (2 lb) Granny Smith apples

Zest and juice of ½ lemon

1 egg

200 g (7 oz) caster sugar

Pinch of salt

A few drops of vanilla essence

30 g (1 oz) plain flour

200 ml (7 fl oz) sour cream

TOPPING

55 g (2 oz) plain flour

55 g (2 oz) golden brown sugar

110 g (4 oz) caster sugar

½ tsp ground cinnamon

60 g (2 oz) chilled unsalted butter, diced

■ To make the pastry, place the butter, flour, salt and sugar in a food processor or mixer and blend. Add the egg yolk and cream and mix together. Do not overwork or the pastry will be very tough.

■ Pre-heat the oven to 180°C/350°F/Gas 4. Tip the pastry on to a clean work surface and press together into a firm ball. Chill for at least 1 hour, then roll out until 0.5 cm (¼ in) thick. Generously line the flan tin with the pastry, allowing 2 cm (1 in) to hang over the edges. Chill again before baking for 15 minutes, or until the pastry turns light golden brown. Allow to cool completely.

■ To make the filling, peel, halve and core the apples and cut into thin slices. Toss in the lemon juice and zest.

■ Whisk together the egg and sugar. Add the salt, vanilla essence and flour and gently whisk until just incorporated. Stir in the sour cream.

■ Add the apples to the custard and mix well, making sure all the apples are fully coated. Carefully place the apples in the pre-baked tart then pour over the remaining custard. Make sure the apples are stacked in a big mound, as they will shrink as they bake.

■ Place the pie in the centre of the oven and bake for 30 minutes. Don't worry if the filling bubbles up and over the edge.

■ To make the topping, mix together all the ingredients and place on the cooked pie.

■ Increase the oven temperature to 200°C/400°F/Gas 6, and cook the pie for a further 15–20 minutes, until golden brown on top. Put the pie tin on a baking tray to stop the base from becoming too brown.

■ Remove the pie from the oven and trim off the overhanging crust. Allow to cool for 1½–2 hours.

■ Cut the pie into wedges and serve with whipped cream, ice cream or Cheddar cheese.

Serves 8

583 cals per portion
25 g fat per portion

Lemon-scented mascarpone mousse with roasted apricots

This is one of those really 'moreish' type of mousses. Use apricots, peaches or nectarines, or whatever soft fruit is at its best.

MOUSSE

2 eggs

150 g (5 oz) caster sugar

2 tsp finely grated lemon zest

175 g (6 oz) mascarpone at room temperature

100 ml (3½ fl oz) whipping cream, whipped to quite firm peaks

2 tbsp lemon juice

Vanilla pod to decorate

ROASTED APRICOTS

12 ripe apricots (2 per person)

Juice of 1 lemon

Juice of 1 orange

4 pieces of lemon peel (use a peeler and take most of the skin off 1 lemon)

100 g (3½ oz) sugar

■ To make the mousse, combine the eggs, sugar and lemon zest in a heatproof bowl. Place over a bain-marie of just simmering water and whisk for 5 minutes. Transfer to a mixer and whisk on a medium speed for 5 minutes (the mixture should double in volume and be light in colour and very fluffy). Whisk in the mascarpone by hand, followed by the cream, then the lemon juice. Place in a clean bowl, cover with cling-film and chill for at least 4 hours.

■ Pre-heat the oven to 190°C/375°F/Gas 5. To prepare the apricots, halve and stone them, then rub a little lemon juice over the cut side to prevent discolouration.

■ Place 60 ml (2 fl oz) water in an ovenproof dish with the remaining lemon juice, orange juice and peel. Add the halved apricots, skin-side down, and sprinkle over the sugar. Cover loosely, but firmly, with foil and bake in the oven for about 10 minutes (the exact time will depend on the ripeness and size of the fruit). When cooked, the point of a knife should easily pierce the flesh of the fruit with no resistance. The juices of the fruit will blend with the liquids in the dish to create a syrup. If you prefer, you can reduce the juices to a sauce-like consistency, by removing the fruit with a slotted spoon and pouring the juices into a pan. Boil down to the desired consistency and return to the fruit.

■ Place the fruit and juices on a serving plate with a scoop, or two, of the mousse. Decorate with the vanilla pod to serve.

Serves 6

426 cals per portion

22 g fat per portion

Soft fruit and mascarpone trifle

Everyone loves trifles, and most people have their own ingredients that makes theirs unique. Our twists to this one include mascarpone for richness, elderflower for tang and plenty of blackberries for flavour and texture. But feel free to use up what you have at home – like biscuits instead of Madeira cake, or raspberries instead of blackberries. After all, isn't that just how trifles came about in the first place?

450 g (1 lb) ripe blackberries
100 g (3½ oz) caster sugar
Juice of ½ lemon
60 g (2 oz) icing sugar
250 g (9 oz) mascarpone cheese, room temperature
225 g (8 oz) custard
125 ml (4 fl oz) elderflower cordial
150 ml (5 fl oz) sweet sherry
200 g (7 oz) Madeira cake
50 g (1¾ oz) hazelnuts, roasted, peeled and chopped
200 ml (7 fl oz) whipped cream
Mint sprigs to decorate

■ Remove the stems from the blackberries and set aside 12–18 for the decoration. Purée 225 g (8 oz) of the remaining berries in a blender with the sugar and lemon juice, then pass through a fine sieve. Toss the purée with the remaining berries and set aside.

■ Gently stir the icing sugar into the mascarpone, then carefully stir in the custard, a spoonful at a time to prevent lumps forming. Set aside.

■ Mix the elderflower cordial with the sherry. Cut the Madeira cake into pieces and toss them into the sherry mixture so the cake absorbs all the liquid.

■ To assemble the trifles, place about 1 tbsp of the softened cake in the bottom of each glass. Top with a generous spoonful of the berry purée (reserving some to drizzle on top of each trifle), followed by a generous spoonful of the custard mixture. Sprinkle on a few chopped hazelnuts and repeat the layers. If you're making these trifles a day in advance, cover with cling-film at this stage and chill in the fridge.

■ Just before serving, top each trifle with whipped cream and decorate with the reserved purée. Scatter a few chopped hazelnuts over the top and decorate with the mint sprigs and reserved blackberries.

Serves 6
722 cals per portion
45 g fat per portion

Figs poached in zinfandel with a mascarpone cream

Fresh figs served warm in a wine syrup make a wonderful autumn dessert for a dinner party. This dessert goes very well with biscotti (sometimes sold as cantucci), the craggy little aniseed-flavoured biscuits that Florentines love to dip in sweet wine.

1 bottle Zinfandel red wine (or another full-bodied red)
350 g (12 oz) granulated sugar
2 slices lemon
2 slices orange
½ vanilla pod
12 ripe figs, halved
200 g (7 oz) mascarpone cheese
200 ml (7 fl oz) whipping cream, whipped to soft peaks
80–120 g (3–4 oz) caster sugar
Biscotti to serve

■ Bring the red wine to the boil over a medium high heat and boil to reduce by half. Add 350 ml (12 fl oz) water, the granulated sugar, lemon and orange slices and the vanilla pod. Return to the boil.

■ Lower the figs gently into the liquid until they are submerged. Lay a piece of greaseproof paper directly on top of them and poach for about 5 minutes. Remove the saucepan from the heat and leave the figs to cool in the syrup.

■ Strain off the syrup, return it to the boil and cook to reduce by half again to give a more intensely flavoured sauce. Pour the reduced syrup back over the figs and leave them overnight, if possible, in the fridge to infuse.

■ To serve, work the mascarpone cheese in a large mixing bowl with the back of a wooden spoon to soften it, then fold in the whipped cream and sweeten to taste with the sugar. Warm the figs through on the stove or in a microwave without letting them boil.

■ Put 3 figs on each plate with a little of the sauce and a good dollop of the mascarpone cream and, if you like, some biscotti biscuits, whole or crumbled.

Serves 4
1,017 cals per portion
43 g fat per portion

Above: Figs poached in zinfandel page 153

Opposite: Date and mocca pudding page 156

Coconut cream page 157

Date and mocca pudding with butterscotch sauce

These sticky little puddings will keep for a couple of days wrapped in cling-film in the fridge. Return them to room temperature and make the sauce when you are ready to serve.

200 g (7 oz) fresh dates, stoned and finely chopped
175 g (6 oz) self-raising flour
1 tsp baking soda
1 tsp vanilla essence
1 tbsp Camp coffee essence
100 ml (3½ fl oz) milk
75 g (3 oz) butter
150 g (5 oz) caster sugar
2 eggs, lightly mixed together
Chopped fresh dates and sifted icing sugar to decorate

BUTTERSCOTCH SAUCE
45 g (1¾ oz) butter
8 tbsp soft brown sugar
200 ml (7 fl oz) whipping cream
1 tbsp vanilla essence

■ Pre-heat the oven to 180°C/350°F/Gas 4, and grease 6 x 175ml (6 fl oz) timbale moulds or teacups. Pour 175 ml (6 fl oz) boiling water over the chopped dates and set aside to cool. Sift together the flour and baking soda. Add the vanilla and coffee essences to the milk.

■ Cream together the butter and caster sugar with an electric beater until light and fluffy. Add the eggs, a little at a time, beating well between each addition.

■ Fold in the flour mixture and flavoured milk by hand in alternate batches, then pour in the dates and their soaking liquid. Ladle the mixture into the moulds, then stand them on a baking sheet and bake in the centre of the oven for about 30 minutes until they are just firm and starting to pull away from the sides of the moulds. Remove the puddings from the oven, turn them out on to a wire rack and leave to cool.

■ To make the sauce, heat the butter in a medium-sized saucepan over a medium heat. When the butter is bubbling, add the sugar and stir together over heat for about 3 minutes until the sugar has dissolved and the liquid is foamy and bubbling. Carefully pour in the cream, then turn down the heat and gently stir together. Boil for a further 1–2 minutes then add the vanilla essence. Leave to cool slightly.

■ To serve, ladle a spoonful of sauce over the top of each pudding. Decorate with chopped fresh dates and sifted icing sugar, and serve with whipped cream.

Serves 6
628 cals per portion
22 g fat per portion

Coconut cream with marinated pineapple

Many people hesitate to make these creams – or bavarois, as they are known in France – believing that they are difficult. Not so! It's really just a matter of making a simple custard, tossing in some gelatine, then folding in the cream.

390 ml (13 fl oz) can of coconut milk

4 egg yolks

350 g (12 oz) caster sugar

6 tbsp Malibu

2 tsp powdered or 2 leaves gelatine

240 ml (8 fl oz) whipping cream

½ fresh pineapple, about 450 g (1 lb) before skinning

Toasted coconut flakes to decorate

■ Place the coconut milk in a small pan over a medium heat and bring to the boil. Whisk together the egg yolks and 150 g (5 oz) of the caster sugar until light and fluffy. Add the hot coconut milk to the egg mixture, whisking continually. Return it to the pan and keep stirring over a medium heat until the mixture is thick enough to coat the back of a spoon. Remove from the heat.

■ Warm 3 tbsp of the Malibu and sprinkle over the powdered gelatine, stirring continuously. Whisk the gelatine mixture into the custard. Strain the custard mixture through a fine sieve and place over a bowl of chilled water to cool.

■ Whisk the whipping cream until softly peaking. When the custard mixture has cooled and thickened to about the same consistency as the cream, gently fold them together until evenly combined. Pour into individual moulds and place in the fridge to set, preferably overnight.

■ Peel the pineapple and cut into bite-sized pieces. Bring 195 ml (6½ fl oz) water and the remaining caster sugar to the boil. Remove from the heat and, when cool, add the remaining Malibu and the pineapple. Marinate for no more than 2 hours or the pineapple will lose its freshness.

■ To serve, turn out the creams on to chilled serving plates and place the pineapple pieces around and on top of them. Decorate with the coconut flakes and a couple of small pineapple leaves.

Serves 4–6, (depending on the size of the moulds)
782 cals per portion
32 g fat per portion

Exotic fruits in spiced syrup

Apples, oranges, guavas, passion fruit, rambutans, raspberries and strawberries could all be added to, or substituted for, the fruits listed below.

12 lychees (tinned or fresh)
1 mango, peeled, stoned and sliced
1 papaya, halved, de-seeded, peeled
　　and sliced
¼ pineapple, peeled and diced
3 plums, stoned and sliced
2 kiwi fruit, peeled and sliced
½ star fruit, sliced
80 g (3 oz) blueberries

SYRUP
500 g (1 lb 2 oz) granulated sugar
1 vanilla bean, split
5 star anise
25 g (1 oz) fresh root ginger, peeled
　　(or 1 tsp ground ginger)
15 cm (6 in) from the tender end of a
　　stem of lemon grass, crushed (or
　　1 tbsp dried, ground lemon grass)
¾ tsp coriander seeds
½ tsp black peppercorns
2–4 cloves

■ To make the syrup, bring the sugar to the boil in 1 litre (1¾ pt) water, ensuring that the sugar dissolves before boiling point is reached. Add the remaining syrup ingredients and leave to infuse off the heat. You may prefer to strain the syrup, but some of the whole spices such as the star anise, coriander seeds and peppercorns can be used to decorate the dessert.

■ Wait until the syrup is cold before adding the prepared fruits, aiming for about 175 g (6 oz) fruit per person. Delicate fruit such as berries, kiwi, star fruit and plums should be added at the last minute, and none of the fruit should be allowed to stand in the syrup for more than 2 hours.

■ Serve chilled in glass bowls or soup plates.

Serves 6
442 cals per portion
0.58 g fat per portion

Chocolate and raspberry queen of puddings

This is a rehash of a classic, adding some of our favourite flavours!

250 ml (8 fl oz) milk

250 ml (8 fl oz) cream

½ vanilla pod, split

80 g (3 oz) sugar

4 egg yolks

100 g (4 oz) dark chocolate, melted and cooled slightly

6 slices of white bread, crusts removed, cut into 2 cm (¾ in) cubes

150 g (5 oz) raspberry jam

4 egg whites

120 g (4½ oz) icing sugar

2 tbsp caster sugar

RASPBERRY SAUCE

150 g (5 oz) sugar

225 g (8 oz) frozen raspberries

Squeeze of lemon juice

■ Place the milk, cream and vanilla pod in a small pan and bring to the boil over a medium heat.

■ Whisk together the sugar and the yolks until the sugar has dissolved and the mixture is light and fluffy. Strain the milk mixture on to the yolks, scraping all the seeds off the vanilla pod. Whisk continuously.

■ Stir in the melted chocolate, then toss in the cubes of bread and leave them to absorb for about 10 minutes.

■ Pre-heat the oven to 150°C/300°F/Gas 2 and half-fill a roasting tin with boiling water. Pour the custard into a 23–25 cm (9–10 in) ceramic baking dish, or 6–8 individual ramekins, until about two-thirds full. Make sure the water doesn't come more than halfway up the outside of the moulds. Cover the tin with two layers of cling-film and place in the centre of the oven. The custard should be cooked until slightly wobbly in the centre. The time this takes depends on the mould: 30–45 minutes for a large dish, 20–30 minutes for individual ones.

■ Gently heat the jam with 2 tbsp water. When the custard has cooled slightly, spread a layer of jam over the top. It should be about 0.5 cm–1 cm (¼–½ in) deep.

■ Place the egg whites and icing sugar in a bowl, and whisk over a bowl of hot water until warmed right through. With a mixer, whisk on high for 5–8 minutes, until glossy.

■ Pile the meringue mixture on top of the jam-layered custard. Sprinkle with caster sugar and cook at 190°C/375°F/Gas 5 for 10 minutes until golden brown. Leave to cool slightly.

■ To make the sauce, boil the sugar with 150 ml (¼ pt) water. When the sugar has dissolved, liquidise with the raspberries, strain through a fine sieve and add the lemon juice. Place a scoop of pudding on each plate and serve surrounded with the sauce.

Serves 6–8

575 cals per portion

19 g fat per portion

Pot of caramel cream with summer berries

The smooth, rich custard texture of this dish goes perfectly with summer berries bursting with tangy flavour. It's equally delicious flavoured just with vanilla – to make it this way, use only 125 g (4 oz) of sugar, adding it all at once to the eggs, and don't include making the caramel.

270 ml (9 fl oz) milk

270 ml (9 fl oz) cream

1–2 vanilla pods, split

175 g (6 oz) sugar

1 egg

3 egg yolks

400 g (14 oz) summer berries, such as raspberries, strawberries, red and black currants or blackberries

Mint sprigs and icing sugar to decorate

■ Pre-heat the oven to 150°C/300°F/Gas 2. Place the milk, cream and vanilla pod in a large pan over a medium heat and bring to the boil. Set aside.

■ Place 125 g (4 oz) of the sugar in a small, heavy-bottomed pan with 2 tbsp water and cook over a medium heat. When the sugar has dissolved, let the liquid boil to a rich golden caramel colour – a light caramel will become diluted in the custard and will not have a strong enough flavour. Remove from the heat and pour the caramel into the milk mixture – do this carefully as it will foam up in the pan. Return to a low heat to allow the caramel to melt back into the milk. When it has returned to the boil, it is ready.

■ Whisk the egg and yolks with the remaining sugar in a clean bowl until just mixed. Slowly pour in the caramel milk, whisking continually. Strain through a sieve into another clean bowl – if there's a little froth on the top, carefully spoon it off. Scrape the seeds out of the vanilla pod, and stir them into the strained liquid. Carefully pour this mixture into 4 x150-200 ml (5-7 fl oz) ramekins or cups, then place them in a deep roasting tin. Pour some boiling water into the tin and cover it tightly with foil so that it doesn't touch the custard.

■ Place the tin in the centre of the oven and cook for about 30–40 minutes. After this, the centre of each custard should still wobble slightly – it will continue to cook even after it has been removed from the oven. The low oven temperature is

imperative to achieve a smooth creamy texture in the pot of cream. A faster, higher oven temperature will simply curdle the mixture. Remove the ramekins or cups from the roasting tin and leave to cool before chilling them in the fridge for several hours or overnight.

■ To serve, place a pile of summer berries on top of each pot of cream and scatter a few berries on the serving plate. Decorate with mint sprigs and a dusting of icing sugar.

Serves 4

428 cals per portion

20 g fat per portion

Coconut rice brûlée with mango sauce

Clever kids have always known that the toffee-like skin is the best thing about rice pudding. Now it becomes a fully fledged toffee topping on a grown-up rice pudding flavoured with coconut and served with a delicious fresh mango sauce.

200 ml (7 fl oz) milk
200 ml (7 fl oz) coconut milk
120 ml (4 fl oz) single cream
1 tsp vanilla essence
40 g (1½ oz) butter
75 g (3 oz) palm or golden brown
 sugar
60 g (generous 2 oz) arborio rice
2 egg yolks
4–6 tbsp granulated sugar

SAUCE
4 ripe mangoes
55–80 g (2–3 oz) caster sugar
Juice of ½ lime
4 tbsp water or orange juice

■ Heat the milk, coconut milk and cream with the vanilla essence to boiling point in a small pan.

■ Heat the butter and palm or brown sugar in a separate pan until the mixture bubbles. Add the rice, stir over low heat for 2 minutes, then start adding the hot liquid, a ladle or two at a time. Cook over low heat for about 20 minutes, stirring frequently, until the rice is cooked. Heat the oven to 120°C/230°F/Gas ¼.

■ Take the rice off the heat and let it cool a little before stirring in the egg yolks. Pour the pudding into a baking dish and put it into the oven for about 5 minutes to form a crust on which to rest the sugar for the brûlée.

■ Skin the mangoes and cut the 'cheeks' from each side of the stone. Slice and set aside. Cut the remaining flesh from the mango stones and put into the blender or food processor with the caster sugar, lime juice and 2 tbsp water or orange juice. Blend, push through a fine sieve and correct the taste with extra lime or orange juice or more sugar.

■ To finish, sprinkle the granulated sugar on top of the pudding and cook under a hot grill until the sugar melts and caramelizes. Arrange the mango slices on plates, put a scoop of rice pudding in the centre and drizzle the mango sauce around.

Serves 4
568 cals per portion
19 g fat per portion

Millefeuille of sharp lemon curd and strawberries

Sharp home-made lemon curd is a good contrast to the buttery pastry and the strawberries. It can be made up to a week in advance.

3 eggs

1 lemon

115 g (4 oz) caster sugar

175 g (6 oz) unsalted butter

125 ml (4 fl oz) whipping cream

200 g (7 oz) packet filo pastry,
    thawed

450 g (1 lb) strawberries, hulled and
    halved or quartered

Icing sugar for dusting

■ Pre-heat the oven to 180°C/350°F/Gas 4. To make the lemon curd, separate 2 of the eggs, then grate the zest finely and squeeze the juice from the lemon. Put the remaining whole egg, 1 of the yolks and 70 g (2½ oz) sugar into a pan and whisk until the sugar has dissolved. Add the lemon juice, zest and 55 g (2 oz) of the butter, and whisk over a medium heat for 5 minutes until thickened. Strain into a clean bowl, cover with cling-film and leave to cool. Whip the cream, fold into the curd and then refrigerate covered.

■ Lightly butter a baking sheet. Melt the remaining butter, cool, then stir in the 2 lightly beaten egg whites. Lay sheets of pastry out flat between sheets of cling-film, and put a damp tea towel over the top layer of cling-film to ensure the pastry doesn't dry out.

■ Lift off one sheet of pastry and brush with egg white mixture. Sprinkle with some of the remaining caster sugar. Repeat this process twice more until there are 3 layers of pastry pressed together, then cut into rectangles about 10 x 5 cm (4 x 2 in). Repeat until you have 12 rectangles, then arrange them on a baking sheet and cook for 7–10 minutes until golden. Cool the pastry on a wire rack.

■ Just before serving, build each dessert in the centre of a plate. Spread some of the lemon curd on a rectangle of pastry, set a few strawberries on top, then repeat until you have 3 layers. Sieve icing sugar over each dessert.

Serves 4

804 cals per portion

54.99 g fat per portion

Blueberry crumble cake page 172

cakes

Carrot cake page 173

& tarts

Spiced apple sultana cake

A moist and rather comforting cake that's not too sweet, gorgeously enriched by butterscotch sauce. Both sauce and cake freeze well, so you can make them a month or so in advance.

75 g (3 oz) golden sultanas

5 tbsp cognac or armagnac

1 lemon

700 g (1½ lb) Granny Smith apples

200 g (7 oz) unsalted butter plus extra for greasing the tin

300 g (10½ oz) caster sugar

2 eggs

2 tsp vanilla essence

375 g (13 oz) plain flour

1 tsp each baking powder and bicarbonate of soda

2 tsp cinnamon

Pinch of salt

100 g (3½ oz) almonds, roughly chopped and toasted

Icing sugar for dusting

Single cream or crème fraîche, to serve

BUTTERSCOTCH SAUCE
200 g (7 oz) soft golden brown sugar
200 ml (7 fl oz) double cream
100 g (3½ oz) unsalted butter
2 tsp vanilla essence

■ Soak the sultanas in the cognac or armagnac for several hours or overnight.

■ Heat the oven to 180°C/350°F/Gas 4. Grate the lemon rind and set aside, then squeeze the juice into a bowl. Peel the apples and turn them in the lemon juice.

■ Liberally butter a 23–25 cm (9–10 in) springform tin. Quarter and core 1 apple, cut each quarter into 5 or 6 slices and arrange them in concentric circles in the tin. Grate the remaining apples, discarding the cores. Toss the grated apple in the lemon juice and leave to drain in a colander.

■ Cream the butter and sugar until light and fluffy. Break the eggs into a small bowl and stir in the vanilla essence with a fork. Beat this into the creamed butter and sugar a little at a time, making sure it is incorporated before adding more.

■ Sift in the flour, baking powder, soda, cinnamon and salt, sprinkle over the grated lemon rind, then stir all these ingredients into the egg and butter mixture along with the grated apple, soaked sultanas and almonds. Carefully spread the batter over the sliced apples in the tin.

■ Bake for 1 hour, covering the edges of the cake with foil if they are browning too quickly. Lower the oven temperature to 170°C/325°F/Gas 3 for the last 15 minutes of cooking. The cake is done when a skewer pushed into the centre comes out clean. Cool for 10 minutes in the tin before turning out on to a rack.

■ To make the butterscotch sauce, put all the ingredients in a small saucepan and bring to the boil over a medium heat, making sure the sugar melts before boiling point. Cook for 1–2 minutes then remove from the heat and leave to cool until just warm.

■ Dust the top of the cake liberally with icing sugar and slide the cake under a hot grill for a minute or two to glaze the apple slices.

■ To serve, pour cream around each slice and trickle the sauce over the cream.

Serves 10–12

778 cals per portion

42 g fat per portion

Lemon pound cake loaf with gingered rhubard compote

The buttermilk in this loaf greatly improves its keeping quality – in fact, we prefer it the day after making, when the flavours have had time to deepen and settle.

175 g (6 oz) unsalted butter
280 g (10 oz) caster sugar
Zest of 1 lemon, finely chopped
3 eggs
250 g (9 oz) self-raising flour
1 tsp baking powder
Dash of salt
180 ml (6 fl oz) buttermilk
1 tbsp lemon juice

SYRUP GLAZE
6 tbsp fresh lemon juice
175 g (6 oz) icing sugar

COMPOTE
225 g (8 oz) fresh young rhubarb
60–100 g (2–3½ oz) caster sugar
5–10 g piece of fresh ginger, peeled
**Grated zest of 1 orange, finely
  chopped**
Sifted icing sugar to decorate

■ Pre-heat the oven to 170°C (165°C for a fan oven), 325°F/Gas 3. Cream together the butter, sugar and zest in a mixing bowl until pale and fluffy – this will take about 5 minutes. If using a food processor, stop the machine once or twice and scrape down the sides of the bowl with a spatula to ensure it is all mixing smoothly.

■ Beat the eggs together in a small bowl. Add the eggs to the butter mixture, a spoonful at a time, allowing the mixture to blend well. Add 1 tbsp of flour at this stage to help the eggs to bind with the butter without splitting. Sift together the dry ingredients and fold into the mixture by hand, a third at a time and alternating with the buttermilk. Lastly, fold in the lemon juice.

■ Pour the mixture into a greased, lined round cake tin or a 20–22 cm x 8 cm (8 x 3 in) deep cake tin and bake in the centre of the oven for 1¼–1½ hours. To test if the cake is cooked, stick a toothpick into the centre of it – it should come out clean. Remove the cake from the oven and leave to cool for 10 minutes before taking out of the tin. Using a skewer, poke little holes all over the top of the cake.

■ For the syrup glaze, bring the lemon juice and icing sugar briefly to the boil to dissolve the sugar, but do not continue to boil or it will thicken too much. Gently ladle the glaze over the top of the cake, a little at a time, allowing it to soak in.

■ Meanwhile, make the compote: slice the rhubarb into 3 cm (1½ in) long pieces. Place in a small pan

★ Fresh spring rhubarb doesn't need much tampering with, but ginger seems to be a natural partner. If the rhubarb juices seem too runny, though, strain off and reduce to a more syrupy consistency.

over a medium heat with the sugar, ginger and orange zest. (The exact amount of sugar depends on the rhubarb, so taste it to check how tart or sweet it is. The ginger can be stronger or milder, depending on your own taste.) Almost immediately, the rhubarb will release some liquid which will prevent it from sticking to the bottom of the pan, but you may need to stir it a bit. Depending on the thickness and age of the rhubarb, it will cook in about 5–10 minutes. Take the pan off the heat while the rhubarb is still in pieces – it carries on cooking as it cools.

■ To serve, cut the cake into slices and arrange on plates with a dollop of compote and whipped cream. Finally, decorate with icing sugar.

Serves 8
562 cals per portion
21 g fat per portion

Blueberry crumble cake

A simple cake to take advantage of fruits left over at the end of the summer. Blueberries are good, but you could use any berries.

300 g (10½ oz) plain flour
2 tsp baking powder
½ tsp salt
1 tbsp finely grated lemon zest
55 g (2 oz) butter, softened
200 g (7 oz) caster sugar
1 egg
250 ml (9 fl oz) milk
400 g (14 oz) blueberries
Icing sugar to sift
Edible leaf for decoration
Crème fraîche to serve

CRUMBLE TOPPING
40 g (1½ oz) butter, chilled
**50 g (1¾ oz) white granulated
  sugar**
50 g (1¾ oz) soft light brown sugar
**50 g (1¾ oz) crushed amaretti biscuits
  or toasted almonds**
40 g (1½ oz) plain flour
½ tsp ground cinnamon

■ Pre-heat the oven to 180°C/350°F/Gas 4, and grease a 20–23 cm (8–9 in) loose-bottomed cake tin. Sieve together the flour, baking powder and salt then toss in the lemon zest.

■ Cream together the butter and sugar until light and fluffy. Lightly beat the egg then add to the creamed mixture, a spoonful at a time, beating constantly. Fold in the flour and milk alternately. Finally, fold in the blueberries, keeping a few for decoration.

■ Use a food processor on pulse action to mix together the topping ingredients until they form large crumbs.

■ Pour the cake mixture into the prepared tin and sprinkle over the topping. Bake in the oven for about 1 hour or until a skewer inserted into the centre comes out clean. Leave to cool for 5 minutes before removing from tin. Cut into wedges, decorate and serve with crème fraîche.

Serves 8
618 cals per portion
21 g fat per portion

Carrot cake

A Canadian style carrot cake packed with coconut, pineapple and pecans, as well as carrots. The flavour develops if left overnight – but the irresistible aroma means it's hard not to eat fresh from the oven!

255 g (9 oz) plain flour

¾ tsp salt

1½ tsp baking powder

1½ tsp baking soda

2 tsp ground cinnamon

255 g (9 oz) carrots, freshly grated

75 g (2¾ oz) shredded coconut

400 g (14 oz) can of pineapple, well drained and chopped

50 g (1¾ oz) pecan nuts, chopped

4 eggs

350 g (12 oz) sugar

200 ml (7 fl oz) vegetable oil

ICING

225 g (8 oz) cream cheese, at room temperature

85 g (3 oz) unsalted butter

2 tsp finely grated orange zest

1 tsp vanilla essence

560 g (1¼ lb) icing sugar

Candied orange peel, finely sliced, and ground cinnamon, to decorate

■ Pre-heat the oven to 180°C/350°/Gas 4. Grease and base-line 2 x 20 cm (8 in) loose-bottomed round tins. Sift together the first 5 ingredients and set aside. Mix the carrot, coconut, pineapple and pecan nuts in a separate bowl.

■ Place the eggs, sugar and oil in a large bowl and beat with a hand-held electric mixer at medium speed until smooth. Fold in the flour minture, then fold in the carrot mixture until well mixed.

■ Spoon the mixture into the cake tins and bake in the oven for 40–50 minutes, or until a skewer inserted into the centre of each cake comes out clean. Remove from the oven, leave in the tins for 15 minutes, then turn on to wire racks to cool. If you are not icing the cakes, wrap them in cling-film (they can be frozen at this stage if desired.)

■ To make the icing, beat together the cream cheese and butter until smooth, then add the orange zest and vanilla essence. Sift in the icing sugar and mix well. Chill for 1 hour, then if the icing is still too soft, add a little more sifted icing sugar.

■ Spread a layer of icing on to one of the cakes and place the other on top. Ice the top and sides, then store in an airtight container in the fridge.

■ Serve in slices, decorated with the peel and dusted with cinnamon.

Serves 8–10

1141 cals per portion

58 g fat per portion

Spiced pumpkin cake

If Hallowe'en is around the corner, this moist cake is right on the mark. Our kids didn't know it was made with pumpkin, but loved it, so even if you don't like pumpkin, you'll probably enjoy this. Custard laced with cinnamon or brandy tops it off.

250 g (9 oz) plain flour

Pinch of salt

1 tsp bicarbonate of soda

1 tsp ground ginger

½ tsp cinnamon

¼ tsp ground cloves

½ tsp allspice

120 ml (4 fl oz) treacle or molasses

1 tbsp freshly grated ginger

125g (4 oz) pumpkin purée (good quality tinned is fine)

60 g (2 oz) softened butter

175 g (6 oz) sugar

1 large egg

TO SERVE

450 g (1 lb) carton of custard, with either 1 tsp ground cinnamon or 2 tbsp brandy stirred in. You could also use lightly whipped cream flavoured with cinnamon or brandy

Ground cinnamon to decorate

■ Pre-heat the oven to 180°C/350°F/Gas 4. Grease and line a deep 20 cm (8 in) square cake tin. Sift the first 7 ingredients into a large bowl.

■ Pour 120 ml (4 fl oz) boiling water into the treacle or molasses and stir until well combined. When cooled, stir in the grated ginger and pumpkin purée.

■ Use a mixer or electric hand whisk to mix together the butter and sugar. Add the egg and beat until light and fluffy. Fold alternate large spoonfuls of the pumpkin mixture and egg mixture into the dry ingredients. Do not overmix, but make sure all the ingredients are well incorporated.

■ Turn the mixture into the cake tin and bake in the centre of the pre-heated oven for 45–50 minutes. It is cooked through when a skewer inserted into the centre comes out clean. Remove from the oven and cool on a wire rack. This cake is best kept wrapped in greaseproof paper, and then a layer of tin foil.

■ To serve, cut into squares and pile high on a plate. Serve with custard or lightly whipped cream, and dust with ground cinnamon.

Serves 8
309 cals per portion

8 g fat per portion

Chocolate chestnut cake

A rich and decadent dessert gateau that keeps well in a tin for several days. The chestnuts give it a smooth-as-velvet finish and the rum a Christmas flavour.

125 g (4 oz) dark chocolate

200 g (7 oz) can of unsweetened chestnut purée

4 eggs, separated

200 g (7 oz) caster sugar

ICING

100 g (3½ oz) dark chocolate

1 egg yolk

25 g (1 oz) butter

1 tbsp rum (optional)

15 g (½ oz) sugar

5 tbsp double cream, whipped until softly peaking

Chocolate curls and cocoa powder to decorate

■ Pre-heat the oven to 180°C/350°F/Gas 4, and liberally grease a 20–23 cm (8–9 in) springform tin. Melt the dark chocolate in a bowl over a pan of hot, but not boiling, water. Blend the chestnut purée in a food processor to loosen the texture.

■ Beat the egg yolks with two-thirds of the sugar using an electric beater on high speed for 3–5 minutes until the mixture is very light and fluffy. Whisk the egg whites by hand until they are firm and shiny, then whisk the remaining sugar into them and continue beating for 30 seconds to 1 minute until glossy and stiff.

■ With the electric beater on a low speed, beat the chestnut purée into the yolk mixture, then fold in the egg whites by hand with a metal spoon.

■ Pour the mixture into the prepared tin and bake in the centre of the oven for 30–40 minutes until a wooden toothpick pushed into the middle of the cake comes out clean. Remove from the oven and leave to cool before removing from the tin.

■ To make the icing, melt the chocolate as described in step 1 and, while it is still warm, stir in the egg yolk and butter. Whisk for 1 minute and set aside. Whisk the rum (if you are using it) and the sugar into the cream, then fold into the chocolate mixture a bit at a time. Use a spatula to spread the icing on the top and sides of the cake. Leave to set in the fridge for at least 1 hour. Decorate and serve with whipped cream.

Serves 8–10

424 cals per portion

21 g fat per portion

Chocolate cream espresso cake

A dark and sumptuous cake of smooth chocolate and coffee-flavoured cream scattered with crunchy toasted hazelnuts and stacked on a biscuit and hazelnut base.

125 g (4 oz) butter, diced

25 g (1 oz) soft golden brown sugar

40 g (1½ oz) caster sugar

125 g (4 oz) plain flour

1½ tbsp cornflour

Pinch of salt

175 g (6 oz) toasted, skinned and roughly processed hazelnuts

400 ml (14 fl oz) double cream

100 ml (3½ fl oz) single cream

300 g (10½ oz) dark chocolate, finely chopped

100 g (3½ oz) milk chocolate, finely chopped

2 eggs

1 tsp vanilla extract

4 tbsp coffee extract (or very strong black coffee)

½ leaf gelatine or 1 scant tsp powdered gelatine

250 ml (9 oz) whipping cream

4 tbsp icing sugar

■ Pre-heat the oven to 170°C/325°F/Gas 3. Process the butter, sugars, flours, pinch of salt and half the prepared hazelnuts together quickly to a crumbly texture and pat into the base of a 23 cm (9 in) diameter springform tin in an even layer. Bake for 15–20 minutes until golden brown but no darker. Take the cake out of the oven and reduce the temperature to 160°C/310°F/Gas 2½.

■ For the filling, bring the double and single creams to the boil together, remove from the heat and cool slightly before stirring in the chopped dark and milk chocolate. When the chocolates have melted, stir in the eggs, the vanilla and 1 tsp coffee extract.

■ Pour the filling over the base and bake on the centre shelf of the oven for 15–20 minutes until just set but still slightly wobbly at the centre. Remove from the oven and cool.

■ To make the topping, soften the gelatine in 2 tbsp cold water for a few minutes, heat gently to dissolve then set aside to cool slightly. Beat the whipping cream until it forms soft peaks, sift in the icing sugar and mix in the gelatine and the remaining coffee extract. Spread in an even layer over the chocolate filling and leave to set.

■ Scatter the top with the remaining hazelnuts and serve in slices with chocolate sauce and lightly whipped cream if you really want to indulge yourself.

Serves 8–10

824 cals per portion

82 g fat per portion

Chocolate chestnut cake page 176

Chocolate cream espresso cake page 177

Fresh strawberries with a tart of fromage blanc

Fromage blanc and fromage frais are often confused. They are both soft, unripened cheeses and generally quite low fat. Usually, fromage blanc comes in delicate, soft curds, while fromage frais is fromage blanc beaten until smooth. Both are mild in flavour and a delight to cook with.

TART

250 g (9 oz) shortcrust pastry, or 20–23 cm pre-baked pie shell

400 g (14 oz) fromage blanc or fromage frais

4 egg yolks

175 g (6 oz) caster sugar

1 tsp vanilla essence

Juice and zest of 1 lemon

25 g (1 oz) flour, sifted

Mint sprigs and sifted icing sugar to decorate

SAUCE

640 g (1 lb 6 oz) fresh strawberries, hulled and halved or quartered

55 g (2 oz) caster sugar

1 tbsp lemon juice

■ Pre-heat the oven to 180°C/350°F/Gas 4. Use the shortcrust pastry to line a 20 cm (8 in) flan case. Prick the base, line with foil and bake blind in the oven for 10–15 minutes. Remove foil and baking beans and set aside. Reduce the oven temperature to 160°C/325°F/Gas 3.

■ Meanwhile, drain the fromage blanc or fromage frais by lining a sieve with a clean tea-towel and allowing it to drain through for at least 1 hour. (If the excess liquid is not removed, the tart can end up rather watery.) Meanwhile, whisk together the egg yolks and caster sugar until pale and fluffy. Add the vanilla and lemon juice and zest. Add the drained fromage blanc or fromage frais and the sifted flour. Mix gently but thoroughly. Pour the mixture into the pre-baked tart shell and bake in the pre-heated oven for about 20–25 minutes until the centre of the tart just wobbles very slightly. Set aside to cool.

■ For the sauce, purée up to 200 g (7 oz) of the strawberries in a blender with the caster sugar and lemon juice then pass sauce through a sieve. Toss the remaining strawberries into the sauce.

■ To serve, slice the tart into wedges and place in the centre of each plate with some strawberries and a little sauce. Decorate and serve.

Serves 6

534 cals per portion

22 g fat per portion

Marbled chocolate brownie cake with orange-scented cream cheese

This cake takes the intense flavour and texture of chewy brownies and blends it with a creamy cheesecake filling. Both flavours are perfect partners for the strawberries. The result is a rich, luscious dessert that's just bursting with flavour.

ORANGE CREAM CHEESE

225 g (8 oz) cream cheese, at room temperature

1 tsp orange zest

75 g (2¾ oz) sugar

1 egg yolk, beaten

2 tbsp flour

CHOCOLATE BROWNIE MIXTURE

125 g (4½ oz) semi-sweet chocolate

85 g (3 oz) unsalted butter

2 tbsp golden syrup

2 eggs, beaten

1 tsp vanilla essence

75 g (2¾ oz) flour

155 g (5½ oz) icing sugar

A few fresh strawberries, cut into halves or quarters to decorate

STRAWBERRY SAUCE

200 g (7 oz) sugar

Juice of ½ lemon

450 g (1 lb) fresh strawberries

■ Pre-heat the oven to 180°C/350°F/Gas 4. Grease and base-line a 20 cm (8 in) square cake tin (a round tin works just as well).

■ Beat together the cream cheese, orange zest and sugar until smooth. Gradually stir in the egg yolk followed by the flour. Set aside.

■ Melt the chocolate in a bowl over a pan of just simmering water and stir in the butter and golden syrup. Stir until blended, then take off the hot water. Leave to cool slightly, then stir in the eggs and vanilla essence.

■ Sift together the flour and icing sugar and fold into the chocolate mixture. Pour into the prepared cake tin. Drop blobs of the cheese mixture over the chocolate mixture and, using a table knife, swirl the two together to create a marbled effect.

■ Bake in the oven for 50 minutes to 1 hour, or until a skewer inserted in the centre of the cake comes out clean. Cover after 30 minutes so the top of the cake doesn't over-brown. Remove from the oven and after 10–15 minutes, remove the cake from the tin and leave to cool.

■ To make the strawberry sauce, purée the sugar, lemon juice and two-thirds of the strawberries in a liquidiser. Pass through a sieve and discard the seeds. Taste for flavour and adjust as necessary,

Continued next page

Marbled chocolate brownie cake page 181

either with more lemon juice or more sugar, depending on the sweetness of the strawberries. Halve or quarter the rest of the strawberries and toss them into the sauce.

■ To serve, cut the cake into squares and place each on a plate. Decorate with more strawberry pieces and drizzle sauce around each plate.

Serves 8
604 cals per portion

29 g fat per portion

Right: Fresh strawberries with a tart of fromage blanc page 180

basic recipes

Creamy mashed potatoes

Serves 4–6

1 kg (2¼ lb) potatoes
290 ml (½ pt) full cream milk
4 tbsp unsalted butter
**Salt and freshly ground black
    pepper**

■ Peel the potatoes and quarter. Place in a large pan, cover with well-salted cold water and bring to the boil. Simmer for 20–30 minutes, or until the potatoes are just cooked.
■ Drain off the excess water and leave the potatoes in the pan. Cover and steam for 5 minutes.
■ Bring the milk and butter to the boil in a small pan and remove from the heat. Mash the potatoes and then add the hot milk mixture, stirring until smooth and creamy. Season to taste.

Creamy potato gratin

Serves 4

500 g (1 lb 2 oz) potatoes
**Salt and freshly ground black
    pepper**
Pinch of nutmeg
1 clove of garlic, finely minced
**1.1 litres (2 pt) whipping or
    single cream**

■ Pre-heat the oven to 160°C/325°F/Gas 3. Peel and slice the potatoes thinly, about 1–2 mm thick. Place the potatoes in a large bowl and

season generously with the salt, pepper and nutmeg.
■ Mix the garlic into the cream, and toss with the potatoes, making sure that all the potato slices are well coated. Pour into a gratin dish and pat down. Use a big enough dish so that the mixture is 3–4 cm (1¼–1½ in) deep.
■ Cover with greaseproof paper and cook for 1 hour. If you prefer a browned top, place the dish under a hot grill for about a minute just before serving.

Sautéed cabbage

Serves 4

**½ savoy cabbage, roughly
    chopped**
4 tbsp unsalted butter
**Salt and freshly ground black
    pepper**

■ Cook the cabbage in plenty of boiling salted water for 3 minutes.
■ Drain in a colander and refresh in cold water. Drain again, squeezing gently to remove any excess water.
■ Heat the butter in a large frying pan over a moderate heat. Add the cabbage and fry for 4–5 minutes. Season with a little salt and pepper and serve immediately.

Crispy fried vegetables

Serves 4

This is more of a technique than a recipe. Use your favourite

vegetables – ours are parsnip, sweet potato and carrot.

2 carrots
2 parsnips
1 large sweet potato
1 medium red onion
Salt
Flour for dredging
Oil for deep-fat frying

■ Finely slice all the vegetables into 2 cm (1 in) strips. Lightly season the vegetable strips with salt and leave for 5 minutes.
■ Dab dry with kitchen paper and dredge with flour, coating them lightly but completely.
■ Deep-fry at a moderate heat (180°C/350°F) until light and golden. Drain on kitchen paper and season to taste. If not using immediately, store in an airtight container.

Sautéed spinach

Serves 4

**200 g (7 oz) fresh spinach, picked
    and cleaned**
2–4 tbsp unsalted butter
**Salt and freshly ground black
    pepper**

■ Heat a large heavy-bottomed frying pan over a medium heat. Add 2 tbsp of the butter, and when it has foamed and then subsided, toss in the spinach. Keep the spinach leaves moving around with a spatula or by shaking the pan, and season with a little salt. The cooking time will depend on the size of the leaves. Younger leaves are more tender and should take no longer than a minute. The bigger ones will take about a minute longer.

■ Add more butter to suit your taste – spinach can soak up a great amount of it and it adds to the flavour.

■ Season with salt and freshly ground pepper and serve immediately.

Perfect steamed rice

A general rule for cooking rice is to use equal volumes of rice and water – for example, 1 cup of rice and 1 cup of water. Rinse the rice in plenty of cold water first, then drain well. Place in a heavy saucepan with the measured water. Add a pinch of salt, bring to the boil and stir once. Cover and simmer for 10 minutes, then turn off the heat and tightly cover the pan with a lid or some foil. Allow the rice to steam in its own heat for 20 minutes. Just before serving, fluff up with a fork.

Microwaved couscous

Serves 4

You can, of course, prepare the couscous conventionally, following the instructions on the packet, but microwaving is super simple and the results are unfailingly light and fluffy.

1 medium onion, finely chopped
½ red pepper, diced
150 g (5 oz) instant couscous
Salt and freshly ground black pepper
25 g (1 oz) butter

■ In a small saucepan, bring the onion and diced pepper to the boil in 150 ml (5 fl oz) water,

simmer for 1 minute then take off the heat and allow the vegetables to cool to lukewarm in the liquid.

■ Tip the couscous into a bowl and stir in the onion, pepper and cooking liquid. Season to taste and leave the couscous to absorb the liquid and puff up.

■ Cover the bowl and microwave the couscous for 2 minutes on full power. Stir in the butter and serve at once.

Fresh pasta

The Italians use '00' flour (available in some supermarkets and specialist shops), which give a good colour or texture. All-purpose or plain strong white flour can also be used.

285 g (10 oz) plain strong flour
½ tsp salt
2 large eggs, beaten
1 tbsp vegetable or olive oil
Flour for dusting

■ Place the flour and salt in a large bowl and make a well in the centre. Add the eggs and oil and, with your hands, mix it all together, adding a little water if necessary to make the dough soft and pliable.

■ Turn the dough out on to a table lightly dusted with flour and knead until smooth and slightly shiny.

■ In a pasta rolling machine, knead the dough by passing it through the rollers on the widest setting about a dozen times. Continue to roll it out, reducing the setting of the rollers gradually to the eventual thinness you will need. If you make the dough in advance wrap it in cling-film after step 2 and store in the fridge until ready to roll out.

Vegetable stock

Makes approximately 1 litre (1¾ pt)

This is a wonderful stock for adding fullness and flavour to a wide variety of foods, from soups and risottos to polenta and stews. It's quick and easy to prepare and you can use different vegetables, such as fennel, mushrooms, shallots, garlic and even tomato to alter the flavours. A splash of white wine can also give a nice bit of acidity.

2 tbsp vegetable oil
1 medium onion, chopped
½ leek, chopped
140 g (5½ oz) celeriac, or 2-3 sticks of celery, chopped
1 medium carrot, chopped
1 small bunch of parsley
1 bay leaf
1 sprig of fresh thyme
½ tsp black peppercorns
1 tsp salt

■ In a large pan add the vegetable oil and gently sweat the onion, leek, celeriac and carrot for about 10 minutes until soft. Do not let them colour or stick to the bottom of the pot.

■ Add 1¼ litre (2 pt) water, the parsley, bay leaf, thyme, peppercorns and salt and simmer gently for 30 minutes to 1 hour. Strain through a fine sieve and discard the vegetables. Set aside to cool and store in the fridge until needed.

Chicken stock

Makes approximately 1½ litres (2 pt)

You can make a more concentrated stock by simmering until reduced by one third.

Approx 1.5 kg (3½ lb) chicken bones, (legs, wings, carcass)
2 medium onions, chopped
2 medium carrots, chopped
4-5 celery sticks, chopped
1 bay leaf
1 sprig of fresh thyme
4 sprigs of fresh parsley

■ Place the chicken bones in a large pan, cover with cold water and bring to the boil. As soon as it boils, reduce the heat and skim off any froth or fat. Add the onions, carrots, celery, bay leaf, thyme and parsley and leave to simmer for about 2 hours. Skim frequently to remove any froth or fat.

■ Strain the stock through a fine sieve, discard the bones and vegetables and set aside to cool. Store in the fridge or freezer until needed.

Fish Stock

Makes approximately 1 litre (1¾ pt)

This is a very simple stock to produce if you have some good fish bones about.

2 sticks of celery, chopped
1 medium onion, chopped
Approx. 675 g (1½lb) fish cacasses, washed
1 sprig of parsley
1 sprig of fennel tops or tarragon (optional)
½ tsp salt

■ In a large pan sweat the onion and celery with just a little water, about 250 ml (5 fl oz). Do not let the vegetables colour or stick to the pan.

■ Roughly chop the fish carcasses to fit into the pan and add them to the vegetables with the parsley, salt and about 1¼ litre (2 pt) water. Simmer gently for about 30 minutes, skimming frequently to remove the froth and fat.

■ Remove from the heat, strain through a fine sieve and discard the bones and vegetables. Set aside to cool, cover and store in the fridge until needed.

Standard vinaigrette

Makes approximately 250 ml (9 fl oz)

There are endless variations for vinaigrettes and a lot of what goes into one largely depends on the kind of dish it is dressing and personal taste. A good ratio to work from is 1 part vinegar to 4-5 parts oil.

½ tsp salt
½ tsp freshly ground black pepper
2-4 tbsp white wine vinegar
240 ml (8 fl oz) olive oil or Vegetable oil
2 tsp Dijon mustard

■ Dissolve the salt in the vinegar with the pepper and mustard in a small bowl. Whisk in the oil, slowly at first to allow it to mix in, then adjust the seasoning.

■ Alternatively, this vinaigrette can be made in a blender or food processor – simply place all the ingredients together and blend.

■ Store the vinaigrette in the fridge if not being used immediately.

Shortcrust pastry

Makes enough for 2 x 22-4 cm (8½-9½ in) tarts

This is a very workable pastry, tender and delicately crisp. Try not to work it too much as the more handling it gets, the tougher the end result will be.

370 g (13 oz) soft flour
85 g (3 oz) sugar
175 g (6½ oz) unsalted butter, chilled and diced
1 egg
2 tbsp cream (or water)
Pinch of salt

■ Place the flour, sugar and butter in a blender or food processor and mix until they form an even, crumbly texture. Add the egg and cream and mix until it starts to bind the mixture together.

■ Turn the mixture out on to a lightly floured surface, work into a ball with the heel of your hand and separate into 2 equal portions. Wrap in plastic and chill for at least 30 minutes before using. The pastry will keep in the fridge for about 1 week or in the freezer for about 1 month.

■ To use, place the ball of dough on to a lightly floured surface. Work the dough out with a rolling pin to form a flattened circle, dusting with flour to prevent the dough sticking to the rolling pin or table. If lining a tart tin, the pastry is usually taken to a thickness of about 4-5 mm. It's also a good idea to chill the lined tin for at least 30 minutes to let the dough 'rest' before baking.

The metric and imperial equivalents used in this book may differ between recipes. For example 5 oz may in one case be given as 140 g and in another as 150 g. This occurs in order to keep proportions of ingredient amounts correct within each individual recipe. Thus, when using a recipe you should follow the amounts given, keeping to either the metric or the imperial list, and not mix the two systems.

Standard cup conversion chart

A standard cup measure of a dry or solid ingredient will vary in weight depending on the type of ingredient. A standard cup of liquid is the same volume for any type of liquid. Use the following chart when converting standard cup measures to grams (weight) or millilitres (volume).

WEIGHT

Standard Cup	Fine Powder (ex. flour)	Grain (ex. rice)	Granular (ex. sugar)	Liquid Solids (ex. butter)	Liquid (ex. milk)
1	140 g	150 g	190 g	200 g	240 ml
¾	105 g	113 g	143 g	150 g	180 ml
⅔	93 g	100 g	125 g	133 g	160 ml
½	70 g	75 g	95 g	100 g	120 ml
⅓	47 g	50 g	63 g	67 g	80 ml
¼	35 g	38 g	48 g	50 g	60 ml
⅛	18 g	19 g	24 g	25 g	30 ml

VOLUME

	¼ tsp		1 ml
	½ tsp		2 ml
	1 tsp		5 ml
	3 tsp	1 tbsp	15 ml
⅛ cup		2 tbsp	30 ml
¼ cup		4 tbsp	60 ml
⅓ cup		5⅓ tbsp	80 ml
½ cup		8 tbsp	120 ml
⅔ cup		10⅔ tbsp	160 ml
¾ cup		12 tbsp	180 ml
1 cup		16 tbsp	240 ml
2 cups		1 pt	480 ml
4 cups		1 qt	960 ml

index